MW00646954

JAMES GARFIELD
& the Civil War

JAMES GARFIELD
& the Civil War

FOR OHIO AND THE UNION

To Mr. Dolan

DANIEL J. VERMILYA

from a lifelong Tribe fan
Hope you enjoy the book!

D. J. Vermilya

THE
History
PRESS

Published by The History Press
Charleston, SC
www.historypress.net

Copyright © 2015 by Daniel J. Vermilya
All rights reserved

Back cover, top: *Ride to Glory: General James A. Garfield at the Battle of Chickamauga, September 20, 1863*, by Amy Lindenberger. *Courtesy of the James A. Garfield National Historic Site.*

First published 2015

Manufactured in the United States

ISBN 978.1.62619.908.8

Library of Congress Control Number: 2015949280

Notice: The information in this book is true and complete to the best of our knowledge. It is offered without guarantee on the part of the author or The History Press. The author and The History Press disclaim all liability in connection with the use of this book.

All rights reserved. No part of this book may be reproduced or transmitted in any form whatsoever without prior written permission from the publisher except in the case of brief quotations embodied in critical articles and reviews.

For my parents

"If I were giving a young man advice as to how he might succeed in life, I would say to him, pick out a good father and mother, and begin life in Ohio."
—Wilbur Wright

"Whatever you do, do all to the glory of God."
—1 Corinthians 10:31

Contents

Acknowledgements

There are many individuals who I would like to thank for their help and support while I have worked on this project. The staff at the James A. Garfield National Historic Site has been wonderfully helpful and welcoming to me. I am proud to have had the opportunity to volunteer for the site over the past several years. It is one of the jewels of our National Park system. Specifically, I would like to thank Chief of Interpretation Todd Arrington, Park Guide Scott Longert and Andrew Mizsak of the Friends of the James A. Garfield NHS. Todd, Scott and Andrew graciously agreed to read chapters of the book for me, and I appreciate their time, feedback and assistance.

I would also like to thank the research staff at the Manuscript Division of the Library of Congress, as well as the staff of the Western Reserve Historical Society in Cleveland. Their assistance has been greatly appreciated. Hal Jespersen was able to bring his expertise to bear in creating maps for the book, for which I am very grateful. My editor, Greg Dumais, and the staff at The History Press have been very helpful in the process of writing and developing this book. Lee White of Chickamauga and Chattanooga National Military Park graciously read the chapters on Tullahoma and Chickamauga, offering valuable insight and assistance that greatly improved the book.

Much like James Garfield, I realize that my friends and family are extremely important to all that I do. My colleagues at Antietam National Battlefield and Gettysburg National Military Park have been a huge help to me over the past year, especially Keith Snyder, Brian Baracz, Matt Borders, Katie Butler, Chris Gwinn, Philip Brown and Caitlin Kostic, each of whom

ACKNOWLEDGEMENTS

ACKNOWLEDGEMENTS

helped me along the way with their support and friendship. My good friend and colleague John Hoptak offered thoughts on each chapter, and his contributions helped to make this a much better book.

My mom and dad each offered lots of support while I worked on the book. It is to them that this book is dedicated. Of all the things for which I am thankful, one of the greatest blessings I have received in life is having the mother and father that I do. I am very glad they raised me in Ohio, just down the road from the James A. Garfield National Historic Site.

Finally, no acknowledgements would be complete without thanking my wonderful wife, Alison. She has spent countless hours reading chapters for me and listening to me talk about Garfield. The only thing that surpasses her patience and kindness is her love, and I could not do this without her.

Introduction

July 2, 1881, did not begin as a historic day in Washington, D.C. Like on many a summer day in the nation's capital, many of the city's residents had thoughts of heading elsewhere that morning. Among them was James Abram Garfield, the twentieth president of the United States. Garfield was still in Washington to attend to some business before the end of the federal fiscal year but was preparing to head out for his summer travels. Garfield's journey from Washington was to take him first to New Jersey to see his wife, Lucretia, and then on to a vacation home on the Hudson River. From there, the Garfields would travel to Williams College in Massachusetts, where the president had studied twenty-five years earlier, to pick up an honorary degree and accompany his sons Harry and Jim as they undertook their own studies at their father's alma mater. James and Lucretia were then to return home to their beloved farm in Mentor, Ohio. Later that summer, Garfield was to journey into the South, speaking at Yorktown for the 100th anniversary of the Revolutionary War battle there, as well as to deliver a speech in Atlanta discussing racial relations and Reconstruction. Garfield was in good spirits that morning, looking forward to being with his family soon. Sporting a light gray suit, Garfield sat down for his morning meal shortly after eight o'clock. Secretary of State James Blaine soon arrived to accompany the president to the train station for the Baltimore and Potomac Railroad.

As Garfield entered his carriage shortly after nine o'clock, he was in the 121st day of his presidency. When he was inaugurated on March 4 of that year, he was the third youngest man and the fourth born in Ohio to take the oath of office and become president. He was a man who had risen from dire poverty to the highest office in the land. His journey through life had taken him to many stations: student, teacher, college president, army officer, state senator and congressman. When Garfield arrived at the train station that morning, he was a man with many miles under his feet and more accomplishments than could ever have been expected of someone born in the rural backwoods of the former Western Reserve in Ohio.

Garfield and Blaine arrived at the station just ten minutes before the president's train was scheduled to depart. As the two men entered the building, two loud gunshots suddenly echoed through the room. Screams and commotion filled the station as the president crumpled to the floor in pain. James Garfield had been shot twice: once in the right arm and once in the back.

The shooter was a deranged man in his late thirties named Charles Guiteau. He was not unlike other presidential assassins, driven in part by politics, jealousy and the desire for a government job, but above all else by an altered sense of reality and sanity. As Garfield lay on the train station floor, vomiting and losing blood rapidly, Guiteau was quickly apprehended and taken into custody. Guiteau believed he was doing the country a service by slaying the president who, in his mind, was part of the corrupt spoils system. As evidence of his insanity, before the shooting, Guiteau had gone to the jail where he would be held in order to see his future cell. He was tried, found guilty and hanged on June 30, 1882, just days before the one-year anniversary of the event.

For the wounded president, the days ahead were difficult. He was taken back to the Executive Mansion, where he would lie in bed and suffer immensely. The summer heat, his painful wounds and growing infection caused extreme misery, vomiting, weight loss and high fevers. Dr. Doctor Bliss (he was a doctor whose first name was Doctor) took charge of Garfield's medical care. The wound was continuously probed in order to find the bullet, a task never accomplished.

By September, the president was still lingering and fighting for his life. To ease his pain, plans were made to send him by rail to the seashore town of Elberon, New Jersey. It was thought that fresh air would help him in his recovery. Upon arrival there, the sea air and ocean view did lift Garfield's spirits, but not for long. On September 19, 1881, after weeks of agonizing suffering, President Garfield died at the age of forty-nine.

For many Americans today who know the name James Garfield, the above storyline is likely all that is recognized. Garfield is not famous for

The assassination of James Garfield, July 2, 1881. *Library of Congress.*

being commander-in-chief during a time of war, nor is he well known for sweeping domestic and social reforms that dramatically impacted the nation. Instead, he shares the dubious distinction of being assassinated in office, joining the grim ranks of Abraham Lincoln, William McKinley and John F. Kennedy. His presidency lasted just two hundred days, the second-shortest term of any U.S. president, behind only the thirty-one-day tenure of William Henry Harrison. Of the forty-four men who have held the highest office in the land, only Kennedy died at a younger age than Garfield.

While Garfield is best known for the tragic story of his death, the story of how he lived is fascinating, heroic and relatively unknown. When he lived, he was industrious, eloquent, passionate and highly intelligent. The story of James A. Garfield is much more than that of a man cut down in his prime by a crazed assassin; it is one of a self-made man rising through society.

Perhaps the most important part of Garfield's rise to greatness occurred during some of the most trying times in American history. Eighteen years to the day before James Garfield died in New Jersey, the nation was in the midst of the Civil War, a conflict that brought death and suffering to the homes of thousands. On September 19, 1863, a great battle of that war raged in northern Georgia, just south of the Tennessee state line. One of the largest and bloodiest battles of the Civil War, the Battle of Chickamauga had a combined casualty toll of over thirty-four thousand. Only Gettysburg had a higher number of killed, wounded and missing. In the midst of this fight and its unfathomable terrors was the man who would one day become president. Eighteen years to the day before he succumbed to the effects of a mad man's bullet, Brigadier General James Garfield was the chief of staff for the Army of the Cumberland, assisting Major General William Rosecrans in administering, organizing and leading that force at the Battle of Chickamauga. In one of the key battles of the western theater of the Civil War, Garfield played an important role.

The fight at Chickamauga was just one part of Garfield's accomplished Civil War career. In 1861, as a state senator in Ohio, he raised a regiment of soldiers that became the 42nd Ohio Volunteer Infantry, a group that served bravely and gained fame on many fields of the war. In 1862, Garfield led Union soldiers to victory on a cold January day in Kentucky, commanded a brigade of soldiers on the second day of the Battle of Shiloh, suffered greatly from illnesses during the hot summer months and sat on a prominent court-martial hearing involving some of the key figures of the Civil War. In 1863, upon taking his post with the Army of the Cumberland, Garfield helped to orchestrate a major Union advance through central Tennessee in the Tullahoma Campaign. At Chickamauga, Garfield bravely served his army and his country, relaying messages between Rosecrans and commanders on the field even as Union lines dissolved in the midst of a withering Confederate assault. For the last two years of the war, Garfield represented his district in Ohio in the United States House of Representatives, the position from which he was elected president in 1880.

An Ohio state senator when the war began, Garfield believed strongly in the cause of the Union and in abolishing slavery. Indeed, by donning the Federal uniform during the war, Garfield was serving both Ohio and the Union, protecting the liberties of his home state while strengthening freedom throughout the nation. In 1861, Garfield was among the first to realize the changes that the war would bring. Even before he had joined the army, Garfield knew that the war would become a revolutionary struggle for the future of freedom in the United States.

Yet despite his having accomplished so much, the story of Garfield's military career is not well known. While books have been written chronicling the Civil War service of other future presidents such as Ulysses S. Grant, Rutherford B. Hayes and William McKinley, none has been written about Garfield's Civil War years. Garfield's story—while little known—is a fascinating journey involving some of the key events and the most important figures of the Civil War.

This book was written to focus on a story line that is all but forgotten in the annals of Civil War history. Over the past year, whenever I have mentioned to someone that I was writing a book on Garfield's Civil War service, the response I have received has almost always been the same: "What did he do?" or "I've never heard anything about that." Even for those who frequent Civil War battlefields, Garfield's actions during the war remain a mystery. This book seeks to rectify that. It is my goal with this book to shed new light on what is an extremely important chapter in James Garfield's life. Simply put, this book tells the story of how James Garfield served his country during the American Civil War.

While Garfield's military service is the central theme of the book, it also discusses his life before the war and how the war and the issues surrounding it gave birth to his political career. It is no surprise that in the forty years after the conflict, every man to win a presidential election, save Grover Cleveland, had fought for the Union. Grant, Hayes, Garfield, Harrison and McKinley were all Ohio-born Republicans, each one of whom had his life forever changed by his military career. In each case, serving in the war was what helped to catapult him into the highest office in the land. In order to understand Garfield—one of the most remarkable men that this country produced in the nineteenth century—one must understand how his life was shaped by the Civil War.

Seeing Garfield only as a victim of a tragic assassination is leaving out one of the most important and significant parts of his life. He was one of many Ohioans who stepped forward to play a prominent role during the tumultuous years of the Civil War, and as a result, he would one day be among those elected to serve as president of the United States. His rise through the positions of life from a schoolteacher to a general to a congressman to a president was absolutely remarkable, and the Civil War was essential to his life story.

I have long been fascinated by James Garfield. I grew up in the same part of Ohio as he did, the old Western Reserve. The first home I lived in as a child was along the banks of the Chagrin River, the same waterway in which Garfield was baptized at the age of eighteen. My hometown of Kirtland is just a few miles away from Chesterland, where Garfield attended the Geauga Seminary. I have lived most of my life within a twenty-minute drive of the James A. Garfield home in Mentor, Ohio, now administered by the fine staff of the National Park Service. Garfield's story has always been inspiring to me. He was a self-made man who rose from the poverty of a log cabin to the rank of major general and then on to the halls of Congress and to the office of president of the United States. The tragic manner of his death does not detract from the heroism he displayed throughout his life, especially during those years of the Civil War when he donned his country's uniform and fought in its defense. Garfield lived the type of life made possible only by the Union he fought to save—and ultimately, the Union he was elected to lead. This book seeks to tell an important and mostly forgotten part of his story.

CHAPTER 1
Son of the Western Reserve

NOVEMBER 1831–JANUARY 1860

The world talks about self-made men. Every man that is made at all is self made.
—James A. Garfield

L ike so many whose names would enter into the history books during the American Civil War, James Garfield came from inauspicious and humble beginnings. His parents—Abram and Eliza Garfield—moved from New England to the backwoods region of northeast Ohio in 1820, shortly after their marriage. Twenty-two and nineteen, respectively, Abram and Eliza were leaving family behind and starting a new adventure. In the early days of western expansion, this part of Ohio had been claimed by Connecticut as the Western Reserve. Just south of Lake Erie, the land of the Western Reserve ran from the western border of Pennsylvania to a line 120 miles to the west, going as far south as present-day Youngstown, Ohio. Connecticut continued to hold over three million acres of land in the Western Reserve until 1800, when the land was formally handed over to the federal government, becoming part of the Northwest Territory. This territory was auspicious for several reasons, most notably because the U.S. Congress, in one of its first and most important official actions, officially banned slavery from the region with the Northwest Ordinance. In 1803— just seventeen years before Abram and Eliza arrived there—Ohio had enough settlers to become the seventeenth state in the Union. The Garfield family settled near the Cuyahoga River, and their first years in Ohio were spent fighting off sickness and raising several children. By 1830, the family had purchased twenty acres of land in Orange Township, a small village with just over three hundred residents, located on the cusp of the Chagrin River Valley.[1]

It was here where, on November 19, 1831, James Abram Garfield was born. Named for an earlier child who had died when only two, young James entered life with both health and size. "James A. was the largest Babe I ever had," Eliza would later note. "He looked like a red Irishman." James was the fifth child for Abram and Eliza. While his namesake, James Ballou, died in 1829, Mehitabel, Thomas and Mary had all survived infancy and the perils of frontier life. Much like his siblings, James Abram was born in a log cabin and into a world and lifestyle that was far from privileged and easy. In 1831, the largest city in the former Western Reserve was Cleveland, with a population of just over one thousand people. The Garfield family did not have the benefits of wealth or prestige; rather, they relied on a strong, industrious patriarch who labored to ensure his family's safety and success. "Your father would do as much work in one day as any man would in two," Eliza wrote to James years later.[2]

Unfortunately, due to a cruel twist of fate, Abram's hard work and support would not last for long. In 1833, he fell gravely ill after an arduous day working outdoors. According to most accounts, he had been fighting a forest fire that threatened his family's land, and afterward he had a "violent cold," which was most likely a form of pneumonia. Despite the efforts of a local doctor, within a few days, Abram Garfield was dead. His death left thirty-one-year-old Eliza behind with four young children. The young widow was to carry out the jobs of mother, farmer, seamstress, educator, cobbler and whatever else was necessary around the homestead.[3]

Growing up under these circumstances made things difficult for the Garfield children, but James managed to avoid the worst of the burden due to his young age. His mother described him as "a very good natured child" but one who was "[a]lways uneasy, very quick to learn, he was rather lazy, did not like to work the best that ever was." Instead of work, James much preferred the outdoors and hunting as he gained in size and strength.[4]

Even more than the outdoors, James had a passion for books and reading, something that would come to have a dominating and determining influence on his life. While he received some education in a small one-room schoolhouse, it was his readings at home that truly captured his attention. The King James Bible and history books about the American Revolution were captivating reads for the young Garfield, but fiction held a particular sway with him. It was reading that helped to expand Garfield's mind, opening up new hopes, possibilities and expectations. When he was sixteen, it was no longer enough for him simply to read of other places. Finding his life at home boring and tedious, in 1848, Garfield said goodbye to his mother and headed for the city to make his own way.[5]

James first went to Cleveland, where he intended to begin a life as a sailor on the Great Lakes. After being rudely and profanely rejected by the captain of a ship, James turned his hopes from traveling the Great Lakes to working on a canalboat. That August, James came aboard the *Evening Star*, journeying in between Cleveland and Pittsburgh. Despite being a strong and healthy sixteen-year-old, Garfield's six-week tenure provided a stern and cold lesson of reality: he fell into the water over a dozen times, fought with other crew members and by October had come down with a terrible illness. James returned home to his mother, who took him in and helped him back to health. After a brief stint away from home, James had experienced his share of rough-and-tumble living for the time being. Having failed his first test in the real world, James would soon begin a different path.

"Sleeping Thunder"

In early 1849, putting his canal experiences behind him, seventeen-year-old James Garfield journeyed to Chester, Ohio, on the other side of the Chagrin River Valley, where he enrolled in the Geauga Seminary, one of several local schools that offered an advanced level of study for those who sought more than a one-room schoolhouse. Founded by Free Will Baptists, the school taught basics such as Latin, algebra and grammar. Because of his family's poor financial state, Garfield worked as a carpenter to pay for his tuition, room and board. He ate a spartan diet, and his few clothing items were exceedingly threadbare and worn. By the time he turned eighteen, Garfield had begun teaching at a district school in Solon to help support himself.

Such obstacles would have overcome many, but this was nothing new for Garfield. He had grown up with nothing but the essentials, and his father and mother had provided him with two examples of how to work faithfully and industriously. James took these lessons to heart, and because of it, these times were crucial to forming him into the man who just fifteen years later would be a major general in the Union army. It was also here at the Geauga Seminary where Garfield first met Lucretia Rudolph, a fellow student who would play a large role in his future.[6]

Major events soon began to transpire in Garfield's life, furthering him along his path toward notoriety and prominence. In March 1850, he attended a camp meeting for the Disciples of Christ, a new branch of Christianity that arose during the Second Great Awakening of the mid-1800s. Sometimes referred to as Campbellites, after the preacher Alexander Campbell, the adherents of this faith believed strongly in forgoing worldly affairs such as politics. Instead, they focused on living out God's commandments as outlined in the Bible. Garfield's parents had been Disciples of Christ, but until now, he had not given great thought to this message. After attending the camp meeting, however, Garfield was a changed man. The message moved him, and on March 4, 1850—thirty-one years to the day before he was inaugurated as the twentieth president of the United States—he was baptized in the waters of the Chagrin River, rising anew as an affirmed Christian and Disciple of Christ.[7]

For the first time in his life, Garfield believed he was destined for greater things. He began to work more industriously than ever to make something of himself. In his diary, which he started in 1848, he reflected on his recent changes, writing, "Thus by the Providence of God I am what I am and not a sailor. I thank Him." Soon, his diary was filled with ponderings about his life and his purpose. "I know without egotism," he noted, "that there is some of the sleeping thunder in my soul and it shall come out!"[8]

In this spirit, Garfield soon sought out a change of scenery. To the south, in Hiram, there was a new school that had been founded by the Disciples of Christ. The Western Reserve Eclectic Institute, later known as Hiram College, offered a different type of education for Garfield. It was more advanced than the Geauga Seminary, and it was in alignment with his strong religious beliefs. In the spring of 1851, he enrolled at the school in Hiram and began an association with the Western Reserve Eclectic Institute that would last—in one form or another—over the next decade and more.

At Hiram, Garfield was immersed in academics. He spent his days with classical Greek and Latin, geometry, philosophy, geology and more, all of which sharpened his abilities as a writer, speaker and debater. His zeal for knowledge and learning was consuming. Years later, Harvey Everest, one of his fellow students, would look back on Garfield's early days at Hiram and recall, "He did not study merely to recite well but to know and for the pleasure of learning and knowing." On many an evening, Garfield would study well into the late hours of the night, waiting for the lights in the rooms of other students to be extinguished before he would even consider stopping for the day.[9]

Working as a janitor at the school to pay his way, studying at all hours of the day and night, debating others on questions of philosophy and religion—these early years at Hiram saw Garfield truly come into his own. He was developing and refining qualities and characteristics that would help him excel in his future endeavors. While he helped to organize the Philomathean Society, a debating group on campus, he still held true to his Disciple disinclination toward politics. In 1852, he expressed disgust over "the wire-pulling of politicians and the total disregard of truth in all their operations." Garfield much preferred to eschew politics and devote his life instead to God, writing, "It looks to me like serving two masters to participate in the affairs of a government which is point blank opposed to the Christian (as all human ones must necessarily be.)"[10]

During the winter of 1853, Garfield began teaching at the Eclectic Institute and preaching in local Disciple churches. His schedule was exhausting. Most days saw Garfield begin his work at five o'clock in the morning, and he did not finish until nearly eleven o'clock at night. On Sundays, he could frequently be seen preaching in at least two different churches. In addition to these busy hours, he was developing a romantic relationship with Lucretia Rudolph, his former classmate at Geauga who had also enrolled at the Eclectic Institute.

In 1854, his hectic schedule could no longer hold Garfield in Ohio. He set his sights elsewhere for academics and distinction. His search ultimately led him to Massachusetts, where that summer he enrolled in Williams College. It was a personal response from Mark Hopkins, the president of the school, that sold Garfield on attending a school so far from home. Hopkins came to have a tremendous impact on Garfield, and the two remained in touch for the rest of Garfield's life.

Upon arriving at the college, Garfield tested into the junior class. With a challenging course load, he studied the natural sciences and new foreign languages, such as German. His skill as a debater helped him to win friends and ingratiate himself into a new social life. He took part in the campus theological society and listened to lectures from men such as Ralph Waldo Emerson, whose words Garfield described as a "thunderstorm of eloquent thoughts" that caused him to feel "small and insignificant."[11]

Williams College provided Garfield the room he needed to grow in numerous ways, one in particular being his feelings on slavery in the United States, the preeminent political issue of the nineteenth century. When Garfield had been a student in Ohio, he had never paid much attention to slavery or abolitionists. Now, after being separated from the strong Disciple confines of Hiram, Garfield was entering into a new world. In late 1855, he listened to several speeches on the western expansion of slavery into new territories. In response, Garfield penned a diary entry reflecting his deep concerns over the future of the country and the immorality of slavery. "I have been instructed tonight on the political condition of our country," he wrote. "At such hours as this I feel like throwing the whole current of my life into the work of opposing this Giant Evil. I don't know but the religion of Christ demands such action." Just three years before, Garfield had disdained all politics and cared little for abolitionists. Now, he was making the transition from a Disciple of Christ who rejected politics to a man who would one day draw his sword and lead soldiers south to defend the Union.[12]

By the summer of 1856, Garfield was through at Williams. Just eight years removed from his time working on the *Evening Star*, Garfield was a college graduate. In the commencement address delivered that year by President Hopkins, a charge had been given to the graduates to go forward and change the world for the better. "Go to your posts; take unto you the whole armor of God; watch the signals and follow the footsteps of your Leader," Hopkins declared. Adding perhaps an element of grim foreshadowing for what lay in store for Garfield, Hopkins continued, "You may fall upon the field before the final peal of victory, but be ye faithful unto death, and ye shall receive a crown of life."[13]

Now a college graduate, Garfield returned to Hiram, where new challenges awaited him. After resuming his teaching responsibilities at the Eclectic Institute, in 1857, Garfield was made the president of the school. He was well liked by many of the professors and students, and his work ethic and academic background made him an excellent choice to expand the school's offerings. On top of teaching a full schedule of classes, Garfield was now also leading the school. Under Garfield's leadership, students from other denominations began attending the school in increasing numbers.

Garfield's personal life was changing at this time as well. Throughout the 1850s, Garfield and Lucretia Rudolph had gone from classmates in Geauga to friends with a romantic interest in each other. Garfield had pursued others in this time, but by November 1858, he had set his sights on Lucretia. The two were married that month. Many scholars have speculated that Garfield's marriage was a source of unhappiness for him. The couple had been engaged since 1854, and some wondered whether the wedding day would

Lucretia Garfield, future first lady of the United States. *Library of Congress.*

ever come. When the day did arrive, it did so without much fanfare. In time, the marriage would become a happy one, but James and "Crete," as he would affectionately call her, would have their share of trials and tribulations along the way.[14]

"Servitium Esto Damnatum"

When Garfield returned to Hiram, his interest in politics, which had begun at Williams College, continued to grow. So did his interest in matters of slavery and abolitionism. In 1859, Garfield began studying law, intending to work as a lawyer to supplement his career as an educator. He wrote to a friend in 1858, "I never expect to be satisfied in this life; but yet I think there are other fields in which a man can do more."[15]

Garfield was becoming increasingly aware of and involved in politics at a time when sectional fires were burning brighter than ever. The same year he became president of the Eclectic Institute, the Supreme Court issued its infamous *Dred Scott v. Sanford* decision, further pushing the nation into a crisis over slavery. Garfield soon began speaking publicly on behalf of the new Republican Party, delivering stump speeches for local candidates in the 1858 elections. In 1859, with more elections coming up, the death of a local candidate left an opening for the Republican nomination for the state senator from the Twenty-sixth Ohio Senatorial District. Because of Garfield's prowess as a debater and public speaker, several Republican leaders came to Hiram and approached him about the seat. After expressing his interest, the Republican delegates took his name to the floor in their convention, and on August 23, 1859, James Garfield was nominated to run for the Ohio State Senate as a Republican.[16]

The election was just a few months away, and with his typical zeal and work ethic, Garfield threw himself into the task at hand. He delivered stump speeches across his district, addressing the issues of the day. A furor over slavery raged throughout northeast Ohio; that year, citizens in Oberlin had taken a fugitive slave out of the hands of slave catchers, igniting a debate over what to do with fugitive slave laws. Most of the campaign speeches that Garfield delivered dealt in some way with the "peculiar institution" and its consequences.[17]

On October 11, 1859, with a tally of 5,176 votes to Democratic candidate Alvah Udall's 3,746, James Garfield was elected to the Ohio Senate. Five days later, a band of twenty-one men armed with pikes made their way through the night along the banks of the Potomac River near Harpers Ferry, Virginia, toward the United States Armory. Their goal: take over the armory, use its weapons to arm local slaves and begin a slave rebellion against the South. The raid on Harpers Ferry was to be a key moment in the long course of events that led up to the Civil War. While the raid was ultimately unsuccessful—many of the raiders were shot and killed, and the rest were taken captive by U.S. Marines on October 17—their message was clear. Blood was now being shed over slavery. The leader's name was John Brown, and his hometown was Hudson, Ohio, in Summit County, part of the newly elected James A. Garfield's Twenty-sixth Senatorial District.[18]

Though Brown's family lived in New York at the time of the raid, Brown still had strong connections to Hudson and had visited there several times in the previous years. While this geographic connection was Garfield's only real tie to the Harpers Ferry raid, the new state senator still sympathized with the cause for which Brown and his men were fighting. On December 2, the day on which Brown was hanged in Virginia, Garfield mourned his death. He confided his thoughts in two separate diary posts that day. In one, he wrote a long, emotional commentary on Brown's execution, describing it as "a dark day for our country. I have no language to express the conflict of emotion in my heart. I do not justify his acts. By no means. But I do accord to him, and I think every man must, honesty of purpose and sincerity of heart." Garfield noted the admirable characteristics that Brown possessed: "When I remember all this, it seems as though God's warning angel would sound the words of a patriot of other and better days—the words, 'I tremble for my country when I reflect that God is just and his justice will not always slumber.' Brave man, Old Hero, Farewell! Your death shall be the dawn of a better day."[19]

In a separate journal, Garfield wrote the simple phrase, "*Servitium esto damnatum*," which translates as "slavery be damned." He had come a long way from the young student who had once rejected all associations with politics.[20]

One month after Brown's execution, Garfield began his career as an Ohio state senator. Ten years before, he had been a poor student at the Geauga Seminary in Chester, Ohio. He had grown up never knowing his father yet embracing so many of the things that were key to who his father was. He was a strong Christian and a hard worker. While Garfield preferred intellectual labor to physical, he worked just as hard at reading and learning as his father had at clearing the acres of land that the family lived on in Orange thirty years before. As Garfield walked the steps of the Ohio Statehouse in January 1860, both he and the nation were on the verge of irrevocable change. In the aftermath of the John Brown raid, tensions between North and South were higher than ever before. They were soon to reach a boiling point, as yet another presidential election was approaching, one that promised to be more contentious than those past. It was in this setting that the twenty-eight-year-old state senator James Garfield arrived in Columbus in January 1860.

CHAPTER 2

Let War Come

JANUARY 1860–APRIL 1861

I am inclined to believe that the sin of slavery is one of which it may be said that "without the shedding of blood there may be no remission." All that is left for us as a state or as a company of Northern States is to aim and prepare to defend ourselves and the Federal government. I believe the doom of slavery is drawing near—let war come—and…a magazine will be lighted whose explosion must shake [the] whole fabric of slavery.
—James A. Garfield

By 1860, there were more than two million people residing in Ohio, many of them recent settlers who had migrated westward seeking opportunity. In addition to the swelling population, the waterways of Ohio—including the Great Lakes and the Ohio River—had also brought an explosion in commerce and much wealth and prosperity to the state. The year 1860 saw Ohio fast becoming one of the largest and most economically prosperous states in the Union. That same year, the finishing touches were also being put on a new statehouse in Columbus to house the state legislature. The building had cost $1.5 million and represented the growth and promise of Ohio and the Union. It was built of marble and granite, strong as the Union itself, which was represented by the design on the rotunda floor: a sun with thirty-four rays, one for each state composing the Union. Around the rays of the sun ran a solid black circle representing the Constitution, which bound the states together as one. This new statehouse is where James Garfield would first enter the

William Dennison, the governor of Ohio when the Civil War began.
Library of Congress.

world of professional politics, and he would do so at a key time in the history of his state and in the history of his nation.[21]

When Garfield arrived in Columbus in January 1860, he quickly became friends with a number of influential politicians who would help guide him through the next several months—and years—of his life. Among these men was the governor of the state, William Dennison. A Cincinnati native, Dennison was a lawyer and profitable businessman early in his professional life. He was similar to Garfield in some regards; he was elected to office in 1859, he was a fast-rising figure in the young Republican Party and he was outspoken against the institution of slavery. During his one term as governor of Ohio, Dennison played an extremely important role in preparing the state for the crisis of the Civil War. He also figured prominently in Garfield's life by involving him in some of the most important matters of Ohio politics.

One of Dennison's most important allies was William T. Bascom, the chairman of the State Central Republican Committee and a close confidant and secretary to the governor. Because Garfield was new to Columbus, Bascom provided him with initial lodging during his first legislative session. The two grew close, and in the coming years, Bascom wrote to Garfield frequently, providing advice, counsel and support as his career took new and unexpected twists.

While Dennison and Bascom proved to be important friends and allies for Garfield, it was another incoming senator whose friendship was perhaps the strongest, most long lasting and most consequential. Although born in Montreal to American parents, Jacob Dolson Cox spent his early years in New York. He went to school at Oberlin College, west of Cleveland, where he initially planned to study theology and prepare for life as a minister. After Oberlin, Cox lived in Warren, Ohio, and instead of preaching the gospel, he worked as a school superintendent and studied law. By the mid-1850s, he had passed the bar and was a successful lawyer, and he and his wife, Hellen, had several children.[22]

Garfield had first become acquainted with Cox in 1858, when he was traveling and delivering lectures across the state. From the start, it was clear that the two men shared many similarities; they were rooted in their Christian faith, believed strongly in education and were increasingly interested in politics. While they had clashing personalities —Cox was more reserved, Garfield more outgoing—they quickly bonded. Garfield believed that the difference in their personalities in no way impeded this important friendship, writing, "[Cox's] nature and mine are in such singular contrast, and yet with so many points in common as to make and keep us friends."[23]

The most important influence that brought these men together was Republican politics. With sectional tensions flaring across the nation, Cox was gaining interest in politics at the same time as Garfield. Cox was vehemently against the westward spread of slavery yet was not in favor of immediate abolition—his position on slavery was nearly identical to Garfield's. Cox became increasingly vocal regarding slavery and politics during the 1850s, even editing the *Western Reserve Chronicle and Transcript* newspaper. He quickly became an important figure in Trumbull County, Ohio, and in 1859, Cox won a state senate seat in the same election as Garfield. The two future Union generals were motivated to run for office by similar events, were elected to the Ohio State Senate in the same election and represented neighboring districts.[24]

Jacob Cox, one of Garfield's closest friends in the Ohio senate and a future Union general. *Library of Congress.*

The year 1860 brought a wave of change to the Ohio state legislature. Of the thirty-five state senators, only eleven had prior experience in the chamber. Garfield and Cox became roommates, and along with fellow Republican James Monroe, a professor at Oberlin College, the three men became known as the "radical triumvirate," emerging as leaders in the Republican Party. During this time, lasting bonds were forged, as Cox himself noted to Garfield: "This past winter has thrown links about us which will not easily be broken, and both our lives will have a somewhat different coloring hereafter."[25]

Having taken his seat in the legislature, Garfield was quickly introduced to the intricate and mundane nature of state politics. In late January, writing home to Burke Aaron Hinsdale, a close friend and confidant at the Eclectic Institute in Hiram with whom he would correspond throughout the rest of his life, Garfield described his first weeks in office: "My place here is very laborious though in many respects a pleasant one. Having the disadvantage of not being a lawyer I have been obliged to study many things with which other members were well acquainted, in order to act intelligently in all matters. I am thus gaining a good deal of valuable practical knowledge."

Garfield was not yet impressed by the legislature, noting that the work had "thus far been chiefly preliminary." Still, the notion that his words and actions were on a much larger stage was captivating enough. "It calls upon a man to have all his sense and balance about him and ready for immediate use," Garfield wrote.[26]

Garfield soon showed himself to be a powerful voice in the senate. One of the early debates that highlighted his abilities occurred on a measure addressing the John Brown raid. Conservatives in the senate put forward a bill promising that Ohio would not allow future military raids to originate from the state, referencing the fact that Brown and several of his raiders were Ohio natives. Being an admirer of Brown and an abolitionist, Garfield opposed the bill. He was representing a part of Ohio that had sent the noted abolitionist Joshua Giddings to the U.S. House of Representatives for nearly twenty years, and many in Garfield's senate district shared those sentiments. Ultimately, the bill was sent to committee, never to become law.[27]

While Garfield was gaining experience in the senate, the nation at large was heading toward a tipping point in the long struggle between slave state and free. The year 1860 was a presidential election year, and Southern and Northern Democrats were split on issues of slavery and its westward spread. Southern Democrats put forward Vice President John Breckenridge as their nominee, while Northern Democrats nominated Illinois senator Stephen Douglas. The fracturing of the Democrats left an opening for the young Republican Party to take center stage in that year's election.

As a rising Republican in Ohio, Garfield soon found himself involved in the key events of that year. In early May, William Bascom described the importance of the election in a letter to Garfield. Of the standoff at the Democratic Convention in South Carolina, Bascom wrote, "I think every day at Charleston only makes the impossible...more certain and bitter." With the Republican nominating convention approaching in Chicago, Bascom spoke of the opportunity that existed: "Now if our friends in Chicago are wise and conciliatory. I think they have the destinies of the Republic in their hands." Bascom took stock of the field of Republican candidates, dismissing men such as Ohioan Salmon Chase, New York senator William Seward and the oft-defeated Illinois Republican Abraham Lincoln as potential candidates.[28]

Despite Bascom's doubts, Republicans in Chicago ultimately nominated Abraham Lincoln of Illinois. Lincoln served as a key figure for many Republicans to unite around, for he was strongly outspoken against the westward spread of slavery, the key issue that united the young party. Lincoln's debates with Stephen Douglas in the 1858 Senate race had propelled him to the national stage, and his speech at Cooper Union in New York in February 1860 solidified his status as a leading national figure on issues of slavery and states' rights.

Garfield was an enthusiastic supporter of Lincoln and the Republican Party platform. In June, the Republican State Convention was held in Columbus at the "Wigwam." There, Garfield delivered remarks that spoke to the heart of the issues that were ultimately at stake that year and, in doing so, further solidified his own reputation as a fast-rising figure in the party and the state. "The great problem of this generation in our Government is not primarily the slavery question but a grander issue out of which the slavery question springs," Garfield began. He defined slavery in the broadest terms as a relationship based on "the manifest injustice of receiving the benefits of another's toil and rendering him no return." After noting that slave and free labor had been in conflict for generations, Garfield spoke bluntly: "The struggle is upon us and must be decided sooner or later. The strife has been raging all along the line, but the center of national power is moving with the sun and in the west will be the final arbitrament of the question." Garfield believed that the fate of the new western states—slave or free—would ultimately decide "the future glory and destiny of the Republic."[29]

Garfield's speech was a success. Fellow Republicans, politicians and newspapers alike quickly rushed to congratulate him on delivering such a clear and powerful statement of the Republican position. With accolades flooding in, William Bascom wrote with advice for the young Garfield:

> *Huzzah for you! Read the enclosure which was in the* Commercial *today. It but speaks the common sentiment of all who heard your very admirable speech in the wigwam.*
>
> *Now, don't be alarmed at this sudden popularity. I don't deal in flattery, but really that speech short and unpremeditated as it was has appeared to me as one of the happiest and best delivered efforts I have heard for years. Your praise is in everyone's mouth. If you will come down here and make a speech this fall, our boys will gladly pay your expenses. You will have numerous calls.*[30]

Shortly after his acclaimed speech in Columbus, Garfield and Lucretia welcomed their first child together. Eliza, nicknamed "Trot" after a character from the Charles Dickens novel *David Copperfield*, entered Garfield's life at a busy time, and her presence did little to alleviate the tensions that were already plaguing the marriage of James and Lucretia. With a busy travel schedule, countless speeches and a rising political reputation, it was his work in the public eye, not his private family life, that brought Garfield the greatest joy at this time. Thus, while his family expanded, Garfield focused his energies elsewhere.

The day after Eliza was born, Garfield delivered a speech in Ravenna for the Fourth of July. While he used martial rhetoric in Columbus, in his home district he was quick to dismiss any idea of coming conflict over the issue of slavery. In his celebratory remarks on July 4, 1860, Garfield praised the Founding Fathers, harkening to their memory as a means of inspiring patriotism. "There is, deep down in the hearts of the American people," Garfield proclaimed, "a strong and abiding love of our country and its liberty which no surface storms of passion can ever shake." Comparing the bonds of the Union to the country's geography, Garfield declared that splitting apart a nation that was so loved and blessed would be impossible:

> But it is asked, must not the question of African slavery at last sever the bonds which bind these states together? It is true that the war of argument is raging—that even angry threatenings are heard—but does this conflict put in jeopardy your liberty or mine? Is the farmer on the prairie of the West or the pampas of the South threatened in the enjoyment of his life, liberty, or property? Has Maine, as a state, any quarrel with Alabama? Has little Rhode Island lifted its hand against Delaware, or has Delaware broken faith with little Rhody? No! Throughout all these glorious states, the people are quietly and peacefully pursuing their various avocations and making ready to reap the golden harvests of this bounteous year. The politicians of the various states are differing, but this difference is not concerning the states themselves, but is a question of right and policy concerning the management of that which lies outside the circle of the states. Is there one of all these states that would break the bond of the union and deprive itself of all the blessings which it affords, rather than have this territorial question settled contrary to its wish? Fellow citizens, I believe there is not one. And if there were, would not the thirty-two remaining sisters throw their arms of affection around the erring one and bring her gently back again to the sacred circle of home? For myself, I have always believed, and never more firmly

than now, that the union of these states will not be severed. If there were no tie more sacred, the strong bond of interest will still hold us together. Every principle of political economy forbids a separation. No state could be severed, no line could be drawn without ruinous consequences to some great element of material wealth. When I look at the map of our country—when I see the beautiful unity of its physical structure, the exhaustless variety of its natural resources, I cannot but believe that, in the deep counsels of God—when He lifted the continents from the sea—shaped their outline and divided their surface by natural boundaries—it was decreed that here should dwell forever a mighty nation, free, glorious, undivided. Who can divide the mighty Mississippi, and bid its waters flow back to their mountain springs, or who roll back the resistless tide of commerce that sweeps down its valley?[31]

Soon enough, Garfield's message of national unity would be put to the test. The task would fall to him and many others to journey down the nation's waterways, over its mountains, through its valleys and across its plains to ensure that it would remain undivided.

These speeches signaled only the beginning of Garfield's rhetorical efforts in the 1860 presidential campaign. He spoke often throughout the following months, providing momentum for the Republican ticket in Ohio. Newspapers took notice of Garfield's efforts, with two papers labeling him a "rising man." Ultimately, his efforts paid off handsomely for the Republicans. In November, Lincoln won Garfield's senate district 6,672 to 3,998. While nationwide Lincoln received only a plurality of the popular vote, he swept the Northern states and captured the Electoral College and the presidency.[32]

Such a victory for Lincoln and the Republicans meant worry and dread for many in the South. Lincoln had publicly declared his belief that slavery was morally wrong and that he and the Republicans were dedicated to stopping its westward spread. Because Lincoln had been elected without a single Southern Electoral College vote, Southern states believed drastic action was their only option. In December 1860, South Carolina became the first state to secede from the Union. Over the coming months, six more states—Mississippi, Florida, Alabama, Georgia, Louisiana and Texas—also seceded from the Union. These states, in turn, set up a new provisional government: the Confederate States of America.

The response throughout the North was strong. In a letter to Burke Aaron Hinsdale, Garfield wrote about the sobering reality of secession and what it meant for the country:

But the stern awful certainty is fastening upon the hearts of men. I do not now see any way this side a miracle of God which can avoid civil war with all its attendant horrors. Peaceable dissolution is utterly impossible. Indeed, I cannot say as I would wish it possible. To make the concessions demanded by the South would be hypocritical and sinful. They would neither be obeyed nor respected. I am inclined to believe that the sin of slavery is one of which it may be said that "without the shedding of blood there is no remission." All that is left for us as a state or as a company of Northern States is to aim and prepare to defend ourselves and the Federal Government. I believe the doom of slavery is drawing near—let war come—and the slaves will get a vague notion that it is waged for them and a magazine will be lighted whose explosion must shake [the] whole fabric of society.[33]

When Garfield penned this letter, only four Southern states had seceded from the Union. No shots had been fired and no battles had been waged. Few others wrote so grimly and bluntly of the coming conflict in those days. Even fewer believed the secession crisis would lead to the death of slavery in the United States. Garfield was clearly ahead of many in realizing what was in store for the country.

Most Americans in January 1861 still believed compromise between the North and South was possible. Among them was Garfield's friend and fellow Ohioan William B. Hazen. Having grown up near Hiram, Hazen had deep connections with Garfield. While Garfield pursued a career in education and politics, Hazen opted for a future in the military. He graduated from the Military Academy at West Point in 1855 and had seen service battling Native Americans on the frontier. When the nation began to unravel in the winter of 1860–61, Hazen was back at home recovering from wounds he had received in battle. He wrote to Garfield on January 26, 1861, to speak of his hopes for avoiding a national conflict. While acknowledging that the Southern states had not taken the step of secession lightly, Hazen pleaded with Garfield to encourage Ohio to act responsibly, providing concessions to the South so as to keep the Union together. "You represent a portion of the Greatest State of our Union," Hazen wrote, "one that perhaps could now do more to preserve our greatness than any other, for God sake strive to have her quiet some expression of at least a desire to preserve our country. Be fair and just." Concerning the possibility of using force to bring the Southern states back into the Union, Hazen expressed his doubts: "The coercion plans will never do. It would immediately lead to a devastating civil war." Instead, he suggested compromise and allowing slavery to remain untouched in the

Southern states. "We must meet them half way," Hazen exhorted, hoping that his friend in the Ohio State Senate could convey his hopes for a peaceful resolution to the governor and state legislature.[34]

Where Hazen worried over the Northern response to secession, Garfield only became more resolute in his belief that the North was in the right. On the same day that Hazen wrote to him about finding the middle ground, Garfield wrote a separate letter to his close friend and Eclectic Institute faculty member James Harrison Rhodes (whom Garfield frequently wrote to as "Harry"), noting, "I fear some of our decisive, bold measures will be lost in the House by the nervousness of our timid men. In regard to the aspect of national affairs, I am really growing more cheerful and hopeful as the clouds thicken." Garfield was one of only three state senators who voted against sending peace commissioners to the Peace Conference meeting in Washington, D.C., in February 1861. His friend Jacob Cox also voted in opposition. Garfield also spoke strongly in support of building up the Ohio militia, noting that it would be wise for Ohio to act in accordance with its sister states by preparing for its defense. Of those who cautioned against offending Southern secessionists by preparing for war, Garfield dismissively proclaimed, "I am weary of this nervous weakness." On top of his speeches in the senate and his writings, Garfield was taking action as well. He and Jacob Cox were practicing in military drill on the grounds of the statehouse, learning the uses and tactics of infantry muskets. While inside the statehouse they spoke eloquently of defending the Union, outside its walls they prepared to do so with the force of arms.[35]

It was in this foreboding environment that President-Elect Abraham Lincoln made his inaugural journey to Washington, D.C., to take the oath of office and become the sixteenth president. The route that Lincoln took to Washington carried him through Columbus, where he arrived on February 13. Lincoln's visit was marked with fanfare, pomp and circumstance. Thirty-four cannons—one for each state, including those in the South—were fired as the train entered the city. Lincoln made his way to the statehouse to speak to the legislature, doing so extemporaneously. Self-admittedly, Lincoln was best with prepared remarks. Without written notes, he had the tendency to wander around the point rather than driving it home. Such was the case in his speech in Columbus.[36]

Lincoln began by echoing some of the sentiments he had expressed upon leaving his home in Springfield, Illinois, several days before. He believed that the task facing him was greater than that which had faced George Washington, noting that he would turn to "the American people and to that God who has never forsaken them" to give him the strength to rise to the challenge. While he had not publicly addressed the secession crisis in the previous weeks, he vowed to act once he arrived in Washington and had "gathered a view of the whole field." As the speech wound on, Lincoln downplayed the threat of war and violence, noting, "We entertain different views upon political questions, but nobody is suffering anything." Lincoln's speech that day was a mixed effort at best.[37]

Later that evening, at a reception at the home of Governor Dennison, Garfield had the chance to meet the president-elect and his wife, the soon-to-be first lady, Mary Todd Lincoln. Upon being introduced, the Illinois Republican and the Ohio state senator chatted pleasantly for a few moments. Garfield came away with mixed impressions of Lincoln. He found him awkward and homely, as did many, but he also found him inspiring, telling Lucretia, "There is a look of transparent, genuine goodness, which at once reached your heart and makes you love and trust him. His visits are having a fine effect on the country. He has the tone and bearing of a fearless firm man and I have great hopes for the government."[38]

Writing to Hinsdale, Garfield went further in describing the sixteenth president:

> On the whole I am greatly pleased with him. He clearly shows his want of culture—and the marks of western life. But there is no touch of affectation in him—and he has a peculiar power of impressing you that he is frank—direct—and thoroughly honest. His remarkable good sense—simple and condensed style of expression—and evident marks of indomitable will—give me great hopes for the country.[39]

After his stop in Columbus, Lincoln continued on with his eastward journey. Upon reaching Washington and sneaking into the city under a looming threat of assassination, Lincoln was inaugurated as the sixteenth president on March 4, 1861. Just over one month later, the secession crisis finally passed the point of no return. On April 12, 1861, at 4:30 a.m. in Charleston Harbor, Confederate artillery batteries opened fire on Fort Sumter, a Federal fort manned by United States soldiers led by Major Robert Anderson. As artillery fire lit up the pre-dawn skies over Charleston, war had begun. The sounds of exploding shells and a two-day-long bombardment filled the air around the city where the secession movement began, but they spread far beyond, rushing through telegraph wires, across the pages of newspapers and through the hearts and minds of the American people.

It was not long before those shots were heard by James Garfield. On April 12, the Ohio Senate was in session, discussing the business of the day. Suddenly, a senator burst onto the floor, reading the exclamatory news that Southern forces had opened fire on Fort Sumter. The stillness that followed was pregnant with anxiety and suspense, broken by, of all things, a woman's voice calling from the balcony. "Glory to God!" cried Abby Kelley Foster, a noted abolitionist and social reformer. The time for talk was over. As Garfield had noted several weeks before, only the spilling of blood was left to resolve the issues that faced the nation. On that April day, twenty-nine-year-old Ohio state senator James Garfield knew that the news from Fort Sumter portended only one thing: at last, war had come.[40]

CHAPTER 3

To Stand by the Country

APRIL 1861–DECEMBER 1861

It is time for Ohio to declare to all her citizens and to all her sister States, that the prosperity of the Union is her prosperity—its friends her friends—its enemies her enemies—its honor her honor—its destiny her destiny—and whosoever strikes a blow at its life strikes also at hers.
—*James A. Garfield*

On April 14, 1861, the United States garrison at Fort Sumter surrendered to Confederates in Charleston Harbor, ending a two-day artillery bombardment and giving the Confederates the first victory in the war. As news of these events continued to arrive in Ohio, James Garfield was deeply moved by what he heard. That same day, he penned a passionate letter to his friend Harry Rhodes, displaying a firm resolve and staunch realism that were rare in the early days of the war:

> *The war has now fully begun. I am glad we are defeated at Sumter. It will rouse the people. I can see no possible end to the war till the South is subjugated. I hope we will never stop short of complete subjugation. Better lose a million men in battle than allow the government to be overthrown. The war will soon assume the shape of Slavery and Freedom. The world will so understand it, and I believe the final outcome will redound to the good of humanity.*[41]

These were remarkable words. In April 1861, few could have foreseen that the war would lead to the end of slavery, the deaths of hundreds of thousands and the complete rebuilding of the United States. Many in both the North and the South believed that the war would end quickly and that their side would triumph with little bloodshed. No one could have possibly envisioned the slaughter of Shiloh, Antietam, Gettysburg or Chickamauga. And yet, state senator James Garfield was already predicting that the war would be the revolutionary and bloody struggle that it ultimately proved to be. In the mind of James Garfield, the stakes of the war were clear when the conflict was just days old. It was to be a war waged for freedom and liberty, for Ohio and the Union.

Writing to Lucretia that same day, Garfield further expressed his convictions regarding the momentous events at hand. "I can see nothing now before us but a long and sanguinary war," Garfield explained.

> *The wanton attack on Sumter and the surrender of Major Anderson can result in nothing else than general war. When I see the outrageous meanness of the Democracy, and the timid and cowardly course of many of the Republicans, it makes me long to be in the strife and help fight it out. It seems to me, that even in the revolution there was no greater need of men to stand by the country and sustain its authority.*[42]

Garfield's convictions soon became actions. Before the fires at Sumter had cooled, he and Jacob Cox went to Governor William Dennison and immediately offered their services in recruiting and leading Ohio troops in the coming conflict.

On April 15, President Lincoln responded to the growing crisis by calling for seventy-five thousand volunteers to put down the rebellion by force of arms. His words were greeted with enthusiasm in the North and outrage in the South. Soon, four more Southern states—Virginia, North Carolina, Tennessee and Arkansas—joined the Confederate cause, and both North and South began arming for war. Ohio was asked to raise thirteen regiments, each composed of one thousand men, and to send them to Washington as soon as possible to defend the Federal capital. Within days, thousands of volunteers were coming from across Ohio to offer their services to the state and the nation. This scene was playing out across the country, both North and South. Farmers, bankers, lawyers and even politicians were becoming soldiers. To manage these new volunteers and regiments, Governor Dennison began appointing brigadier generals. Jacob Cox was among the first appointed to command the new troops. Garfield hoped his chance would soon follow.[43]

On the same day that Lincoln called for volunteers in defense of the Union, Garfield was in Columbus arguing passionately in favor of Ohio's participation in the country's defense. In February, Garfield had written a bill that would punish treason with life imprisonment. Soon after Fort Sumter, the measure was reported to the senate. In its support, Garfield wrote a strong indication of the passionate feelings that he would carry through the rest of the war: "It is time for Ohio to declare to all her citizens and to all her sister States, that the prosperity of the Union is her prosperity—its friends her friends—its enemies her enemies—its honor her honor—its destiny her destiny—and whosoever strikes a blow at its life strikes also at hers."

Aided no doubt by the events in Charleston, the measure passed easily, much to the displeasure of several vocal Democrats. Also at this time, Garfield advocated for a bill that would fund and equip the militia regiments Ohio was raising. On April 17, in the midst of this fervor, Garfield wrote to Dennison to officially offer his "services for any position in the military organization of the State to which you may see fit to appoint me."[44]

Dennison did have a job for Garfield, but not the type the young state senator had in mind. The governor asked Garfield to travel to Illinois to inquire about five thousand excess muskets in that state's arsenal, as well as to see about consolidating troops from Illinois and Indiana under the command of Major General George B. McClellan, who had just accepted Dennison's offer to lead all Ohio troops. Garfield dutifully made the trip and was successful on both of his objectives, but his desire to serve in uniform still remained strong.

Just before his excursion to Illinois, Garfield told Lucretia that in all likelihood he would soon be named the colonel of the 7th Ohio Volunteer Infantry Regiment, which was being recruited and organized in the Cleveland area. The first group of regiments raised by the state elected its officers democratically, and Garfield believed his reputation strong enough and his friends in the regiment loyal enough to see that he would win the commanding position. "The more I reflect on the whole subject, the more I feel that I cannot stand aloof from this conflict," he wrote. "My heart and hope for the country are in it and I could do no justice to the everyday duties of life."

Garfield, himself a young man, was impressed with the characteristics and qualities that those volunteering were displaying that spring. He relayed a story regarding a company of recruits who had recently arrived in Columbus and spent the night sleeping on the floor of the statehouse rotunda. The same rotunda that was emblazoned with the symbol of the sun representing the

Union now saw soldiers sleeping there who had pledged to defend the Union itself. The men held a prayer meeting and sang patriotic songs and hymns before sleeping on the marble floor that night. The scene left an indelible impression on Garfield, who noted to Lucretia, "Such men will fight."[45]

Despite such high enthusiasm to wear an army uniform, Garfield would have to wait before his chance to lead a regiment would arrive. During his trip to Illinois to carry out Governor Dennison's wishes, events conspired to deprive him of his opportunity with the 7th Ohio. In his absence, Erastus Tyler, a businessman who had lived in Ravenna for several years, rose to a position of prominence and was elected as the regiment's commander. Garfield learned of the news soon after Tyler had been chosen, and the shock was great. He had helped to recruit men for the regiment and was certain that the command was to be his, but his absence at a crucial time had changed his fate. "Myself and many others of your friends exerted ourselves among the men to obtain your election," wrote Henry Spencer, one of Garfield's supporters in the regiment. "Had you been upon the ground it would have insured [sic] success."[46]

The incident was not only a personal setback, but it was also celebrated by Garfield's political opponents. The Weekly Portage Sentinel, a Democratic paper in Ravenna, accused him of being motivated by personal success, not love of country. Noting that Garfield had promised the men of the 7th Ohio that he would join them in the field, the Sentinel mocked Garfield by suggesting, "We presume he will soon enlist as a private!"[47]

Garfield's disappointment aside, Tyler was certainly qualified to lead the regiment. He had helped to recruit a large portion of the men, and his efforts paid off handsomely with his election. He would end up playing a prominent role in the war, serving in the fighting in western Virginia and the Shenandoah Valley, as well as in many of the campaigns of the famed Army of the Potomac. By the end of the war, he held the brevet rank of major general. While Tyler's election was deserved, it was also a direct result of Garfield's efforts in Illinois on behalf of Governor Dennison. There was little doubt that had Garfield not dutifully gone to Illinois on Dennison's behalf, he would have won his colonelcy. Knowing this, Garfield did not take the news well. He believed Tyler had engaged in "treachery" and that his election was the result of "bargains and brandy."[48]

Making his disappointment over the 7th Ohio even more acute was the flood of letters that Garfield received in April and May 1861 from friends, colleagues and those who simply knew he was an influential man in Columbus. Because of his prominent position in the state and his relationship with

Dennison, Garfield was besieged with requests for prestigious appointments and offices. "This is a time when every true Patriot feels rising up within him a desire to aid his country in the coming struggle," wrote J.T. Smith, a friend of Garfield's from Warren who was seeking a position as an army surgeon. Garfield's cousin John Clapp wrote to ask for an officer's commission as well as to possibly sell horses to the Ohio regiments being raised.[49]

Perhaps most audacious was William Hazen, Garfield's friend from Hiram. Despite being a West Point graduate and an officer in the regular army, Hazen sought an appointment leading an Ohio regiment in the war. He asked Garfield to meet with the governor on his behalf and to "try and have some position left for me," especially one commanding troops from northeast Ohio. "I would like very much to engage in this strife if at all with my people," wrote Hazen. Two weeks later, Hazen again wrote to Garfield concerning the raising of troops. He included advice for his friend as well this time, suggesting that Garfield secure an officer's post soon: "You had better get one of these regiments for yourself, or if you are not ambitious in a military capacity, for us go in the same regiment. It can be formed entirely of our own people and I am sure will give a good account of itself. Don't lose track of this matter." Ultimately, Hazen's wishes were fulfilled. He became the colonel of the 41st Ohio Volunteer Infantry, raised primarily from Lake, Geauga and other northeast Ohio counties. Both Hazen and his regiment went on to great fame in the war.[50]

Thus, Garfield's friends and acquaintances—Jacob Cox, William Hazen and Erastus Tyler, among many others—had quick success in finding positions in the army, all while Garfield was still in Ohio doing what he could as a politician and being subjected to partisan attacks on his reputation. Shortly after his failure with the 7th Ohio, Garfield hoped to become the colonel of the 19th Ohio Regiment, but this opportunity fell apart as well. With his frustration mounting, Garfield wrote to John Clapp, expressing worries that his reputation in his home district was being affected: "There seems to be in the community a perfect crazy determination to make it out that I [am] making great exertions to secure a place." With this in mind, he thought it best to step back from his efforts in the summer of 1861. Indeed, when he was offered a lieutenant colonelcy with the 24th Ohio, Garfield turned it down, informing Governor Dennison that "my personal affairs and my relations to those with whom I am in business connection" caused him to decline, although he did leave the door open to taking such a position in the future. His excuse for saying no to the 24th Ohio was more obfuscation than anything else. He was simply depressed.[51]

In June and July, with his hopes dashed and his ego no doubt bruised, Garfield was prepared to remain at home for the time being. He was gripped by a melancholy that would afflict him from time to time throughout his life. Beset by the pressures of his standing in society, as well as the standards he set for himself, Garfield was subject to emotional swings. Making his malaise all the worse was dissatisfaction in his personal life at this time. He had still not warmed to the role of husband, and the added role of father after Eliza's birth had not improved his situation. His unease with his family situation was only compounded upon by his troubles securing a position in the army in 1861. From the heights of war fever in April, he was now in the depths of despair in June.[52]

Meanwhile, Brigadier General Jacob Cox was commanding troops in a crucial campaign to protect the loyal western region of Virginia. In late June, Bascom wrote to Garfield of Cox's success, noting that he was turning out to be "the most popular general on the ground." In the same letter, Bascom tried to lift Garfield out of his depression, adding, "I hope a kind Providence…will also permit you yet to enter the service. There will be other calls and openings before the war is over." As Bascom predicted, Garfield's opportunity would come soon enough.[53]

While the first regiments raised in Ohio all elected their officers democratically, after the 22nd Ohio Volunteers had entered the service, the process changed. Now, it was the governor who appointed colonels, giving greater power and patronage to the state executive. In late July, with more regiments being called upon to put down the rebellion, Governor Dennison sent a note to the state senator from Hiram: "I am organizing some new regiments. Can you take a Lieut. Colonelcy? I am anxious you should do so. Reply by telegraph." This time, the answer would be different. The message pierced through Garfield's malaise, and he quickly accepted this new offer to serve. Just a few months shy of his thirtieth birthday, James Garfield was to be the lieutenant colonel of the 42nd Ohio Volunteer Infantry.[54]

In his reply, Garfield inquired about whether the regiment would be led by a West Point officer, stating that he wished to be paired with an experienced commander. Aside from military texts and drilling with Jacob Cox on the grounds of the Ohio Statehouse, Garfield was entirely inexperienced in military command. This enterprise, though much sought after, was new to him, and having a steady hand to guide him would help him assimilate to this new life.[55]

When his reply was received in Columbus, Bascom quickly wrote back to Garfield, telling him of the necessity to raise the regiment as quickly as possible. In late July, Union forces had suffered an embarrassing defeat at the Battle of Bull Run (soon to be known as First Bull Run, or First Manassas, as Confederates called it). While Bascom did not mention it by name, it was no doubt a primary reason Ohio had "a strong purpose for getting the regiment in the field at an early day." In regard to a West Point officer, Bascom told Garfield that there was a dearth of such experience available at that time but that Governor Dennison would "do the best he can for you."[56]

Despite this wish, there was to be no West Point officer to tutor Garfield in military life. Instead, in early September, he was appointed a full colonel. At long last, he had his regiment, and he had it all to himself. Serving under him would be Lieutenant Colonel Lionel Sheldon and Major Don Pardee, two acquaintances with whom Garfield became especially close as the war progressed. Sheldon hailed from Elyria, Ohio, where he practiced law. He was familiar with the military, having served as an officer in the Ohio militia before joining the 42nd. Pardee was a former student at the Naval Academy in Annapolis and was also well read in military theory. He was a practicing attorney in Medina County before the war and had married just before the fighting began. Each of these officers complemented Garfield well.[57]

Once Garfield accepted Governor Dennison's offer, the real work began. Before he could command a regiment, he first had to raise and recruit one. When he was first mustered in as the regiment's lieutenant colonel, he was the only man assigned to the 42nd. Here, his rhetorical prowess and strong reputation were well employed. Though based out of Camp Chase in Columbus, Garfield managed to cover a wide swath of territory in his recruiting trips. In his journeys, he relied heavily on his prior experience as a minister, as Garfield biographer Allan Peskin has chronicled. The former Disciple of Christ preacher was now a missionary for the Union, exhorting his fellow Ohioans to take up arms in its defense. Often at the end of his remarks, rather than asking those listening to stand for Christ, Garfield asked for volunteers to stand to defend the Union. This style of employing religious fervor in defense of the Union was typical in 1861. While many employed it to recruit, few did it as effectively as James Garfield. His first stop was his old home, the Western Reserve Eclectic Institute. There, he found willing disciples for his message; he spoke passionately for the cause, and his former students became his new soldiers. He raised an entire company at Hiram that would become Company A of the 42nd Ohio.[58]

By early October, Garfield had six companies with him in Columbus, with more still arriving. With his regiment forming, the training was underway. At first, the men drilled with wooden muskets and were outfitted with whatever

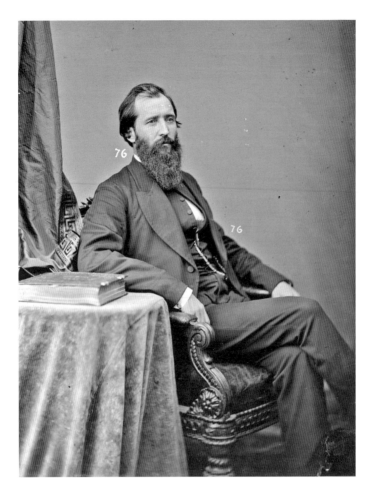

Lieutenant Colonel Lionel Sheldon of the 42nd Ohio Volunteer Infantry. *Library of Congress.*

uniforms were available. Garfield trained the regiment in these early weeks the same way he had trained young minds at the Eclectic Institute in Hiram. He established instructional classes for his officers, and the regiment operated as if it were a class of students studying for an exam. The officers did recitations of their manuals and studied tactics as Garfield had once studied geometry or Latin. Garfield used wooden blocks to teach various tactical maneuvers for his new officers, drilling the men in the ranks between six and eight hours a day. Frank Holcombe Mason, a student from Hiram, described Garfield's influence in the autumn of 1861 as "unbounded." Mason wrote in his history of the 42nd Ohio that few others but Garfield could have had such a strong and immediate effect on so many young men, a large number of whom had previously been students:

As colonel not less than as Professor and Principal of a collegiate school, he evinced a rare and extraordinary power in controlling, interesting and inspiring young men. It was due largely to his enthusiastic efforts that the regiment was made up of some of the best material that Ohio sent into the field. The careful, laborious education, the discipline, the quickening of individual self-respect that the regiment underwent at his hands while in Camp Chase were never lost upon its men. Long after he had gone to other duties the recollection of his words was a source of inspiration.[59]

Garfield himself evinced great pride in his regiment, especially during its formative months. Writing years later, Garfield described the extraordinary process of preparing for the war that was gripping the nation: "It is remarkable with what facility the American mind adapts itself to situations, and this has never been so strikingly illustrated as in the great movements of 1861, which transformed in so short a time so great a multitude of young men from the unlimited independence of American citizens to the willing but severe restraints of military discipline."[60]

In the midst of the flurry of recruiting and training, Garfield received many congratulatory notes regarding his new position. None perhaps was more meaningful than a letter from Jacob Cox, who by that time had already been leading troops on campaign for several months. In early November, Cox wrote to Garfield to praise his work thus far and to hope that they might be colleagues once again: "I am glad to know that your regiment is so nearly full, and I assure you that there is nothing I have set my heart on more than having you with me."[61]

By late November, when the ranks were finally full, new uniforms, knapsacks and other necessities were distributed to the troops. Soon after, the men received their weapons. According to Mason, the guns were Belgian-made rifles, not the Harpers Ferry or Enfield models many had anticipated. As the days grew colder, the men became increasingly anxious to leave Camp Chase and head off for war. On December 14, to the pleasure of many, the 42nd Ohio was ordered out of camp. Owen Hopkins recalled that the moment "was greeted with loud cheers." The men were tired of drilling, and the newly minted soldiers were ready to "battle manfully for the old Flag."[62]

The next day, Colonel James Garfield and the 42nd Ohio marched off to war. When they arrived at the railroad depot in Columbus, they were greeted by well-wishers. Among them was Governor Dennison. The governor presented the regiment its new flag and provided some brief remarks. Garfield later told Lucretia that the governor informed him "that the 42nd was the best regiment that had yet been raised in the state." After the governor spoke, Garfield himself provided a brief piece of oratory, reminding the men to hold on to the flag under any circumstances, promising to carry the colors "through many a sanguine field to victory." With the ceremonies dispensed with, Garfield and his men were soon on a train to Cincinnati.[63]

Along the journey to Cincinnati, the 42nd Ohio was greeted with revelers bearing food for the soldiers. The fanfare marked a tremendous occasion in the lives of the men. They were leaving the civilian world behind and embarking on a new adventure as soldiers. The same could be said for James Garfield. For a man who had worked on the towpath of the canal, taught in numerous schoolhouses, dabbled in practicing law, preached sermons on the Gospel across the state, served in the Ohio Senate and worked closely as a political associate of Governor William Dennison, he was now about to add new titles and experiences to his life's story. He would soon command a brigade of men in combat against an enemy in a dangerous and inhospitable region. As Mason wrote years later of the moment, "The period of preparation over, the real work of the Forty-Second was now about to begin."[64]

CHAPTER 4

Kentucky

I hope to have God on my side, but I must have Kentucky.
—Abraham Lincoln[65]

O f all the states involved in the American Civil War, few were as hotly contested as the state of Kentucky. While eleven Southern slaveholding states seceded to form the Confederacy, there were four slave states that remained in the Union during the conflict. These Border States—Delaware, Maryland, Missouri and Kentucky—were vital to the interest of each side. Of these Border States, Kentucky repeatedly emerged as a top concern for both the Union and the Confederacy. After all, the leaders of both sides— Abraham Lincoln and Jefferson Davis—were born there.

At the start of the conflict, Kentucky declared its neutrality, hoping to avoid being caught between the two sides. Yet the strategic importance of the state meant that it would be almost impossible for each side to ignore Kentucky altogether. If Kentucky joined the Confederacy, or was simply held by Southern forces, then Confederate troops would have a staging area to launch excursions into Northern states such as Ohio, Indiana and Illinois, as well as the ability to control the Ohio River and transportation through the western states. For the Union, Kentucky offered just the opposite; it was a place from which Union forces could utilize the river network of the western Confederacy and break the South's defenses. Keeping Kentucky in the Union meant a Border State barrier between Ohio and Tennessee, something that was indispensable to Lincoln and the North in the early days of the Civil War.

The first months of the war passed as a tense standoff, with neither side infringing on Kentucky's soil. When Confederate general Leonidas Polk occupied the crucial city of Columbus, Kentucky, in September 1861, everything changed. Columbus was located on the Mississippi River, and Polk believed it was an essential stronghold for the Confederacy. Several days later, Union forces entered the state and took control of Paducah. These Union troops were led by a little-known Union officer, Brigadier General Ulysses S. Grant.

Kentucky's governor, Beriah Magoffin, demanded both armies leave his state. Yet Kentucky's legislature, which was more Unionist than the state's Southern-sympathizing governor, called for only the Confederates to withdraw from Kentucky soil and asked the Federal government for help in reclaiming the state. Ultimately, neither army budged on its own, and Kentucky became an important battleground of the Civil War.

For Confederates, fighting for possession of Kentucky was better than seeing the state fall into Federal hands. Defending such a vast swath of territory, however, was a difficult task. From Kentucky to the Mississippi River, Confederates were vulnerable to Union advances on numerous points. Because of this daunting challenge, Confederate president Jefferson Davis placed General Albert Sidney Johnston in command of the Confederacy's western defenses. Johnston was one of the most highly regarded generals on either side in 1861, yet he was vastly outnumbered by the Federals in the West, having no more than forty thousand men under his command. Johnston was forced to spread his men out, occupying key locations and moving them when necessary to create the appearance of a larger force than he actually had.[66]

While Federal troops in this department vastly outnumbered Confederates, Johnston's defensive tactics had an early effect on the Union commander in this region, Brigadier General William Tecumseh Sherman. Years before he became infamous for his campaigns in Georgia and the Carolinas, Sherman was the commander of the Department of the Cumberland in Kentucky in late 1861. Sherman had been reluctant to accept such an important command so early in the war, and the stress of the post was too much for him to bear. In November 1861, Sherman had a breakdown, proclaiming that Confederate forces were too great in number and that the war would be longer and more difficult than anyone could imagine. Sherman asked to be relieved, and he was replaced by Major General Don Carlos Buell. Upon Buell's ascension to command, he combined his troops in the field into a force known as the Army of the Ohio.[67]

Major General Don Carlos Buell. *Library of Congress.*

A graduate of the West Point class of 1841, Buell was an Ohio native who served under Winfield Scott and Zachary Taylor in the Mexican War, where he was severely wounded at the Battle of Churubusco. He was in the army in an administrative post in California when the Civil War began and quickly came east to take part in the conflict. After helping to organize recruits in Washington, Buell was promoted to brigadier general, and in November, he was given one of the most important assignments in the entire army. He was to be responsible for piercing the western defenses of the Confederacy, holding Kentucky for the Union and defending the rivers and waterways that were to play a pivotal role in the western theater of the war.[68]

With his command in Kentucky, Buell was placed in a stressful situation. Union general-in-chief George B. McClellan made clear that Kentucky was an extremely high priority for Federal forces; only Virginia loomed larger in Union war plans in late 1861. Despite the Confederate incursions into Kentucky and the legislature aligning itself with the North, concerns over Kentucky's loyalty to the Union still persisted. President Lincoln himself was insistent on protecting the crucial Border State, writing, "To lose Kentucky is nearly the same as to lose the whole game." Thus, as Buell was told, any Federal operations in the state needed to have the added benefit of encouraging the loyalty of the citizens. This meant that Union armies had to tread lightly so as not to damage civilian property or create any more Southern sympathy than already existed.[69]

In order to hold Kentucky, Buell would have to send Union forces into the state to protect its citizens and repulse any Confederate forces. In December 1861, these efforts would bring James Garfield and his men into combat for the first time in the war.

Garfield's first campaign was to take place in the far eastern reaches of Kentucky, a mountainous no-man's land for the North and the South. The country was rugged and inhospitable for military campaigns. The highest of the mountains here reached over four thousand feet in elevation. Besides these peaks, the most prominent geographic feature was the Big Sandy River, which ran through the Big Sandy Valley and provided a border between the neutral state of Kentucky and the Confederate state of Virginia. Flowing from south to north and ending at the Ohio River, the Big Sandy cut through four crucial counties that would see significant action in the upcoming campaign. According to the 1860 census, there were over 26,000 people living in Lawrence, Pike, Floyd and Johnson Counties at the time of the war. These citizens of the Big Sandy Valley relied primarily on agriculture, with coal and timber composing a relatively small part of the region's economy. As opposed to other parts of Kentucky, this region was far from a bastion of slavery—in the four counties listed above, there were a total of 117 slaveholders who owned just over 400 slaves. A basic road system and steamboats on the rivers provided the primary means of transportation through the area. In the crucial 1860 election, the Big Sandy Valley had gone for Southern Democratic candidate and sitting vice president John Breckenridge. Though these results suggest that the region was in full support of the Southern cause, such was not the case; several Unionist candidates from the area were elected to Congress in 1861.

General Humphrey Marshall, Garfield's opponent in the Big Sandy
Valley Campaign. *Library of Congress.*

In November 1861, an initial Federal force was sent into the valley under
the command of General William Nelson. Nelson's command moved
toward the town of Prestonburg in an attempt to secure the area with a
strong Federal presence. Nelson did not occupy the area for more than a few
weeks before he was recalled. Soon, another military force took hold of the
valley; this time, the soldiers were Confederates.[70]

Their commander was a portly general with exactly the type of
résumé that would demand respect and admiration so early on in the war.
Humphrey Marshall was a native Kentuckian—he was born in Frankfurt
in 1812—who had attended the U.S. Military Academy at West Point,

from which he graduated in 1832. In the 1830s, he served briefly in the U.S. Army before resigning to become an attorney. While practicing law in his home state, Marshall became active in the Kentucky state militia. During the Mexican War, he led the 1st Kentucky Cavalry and saw combat in several engagements, including the Battle of Buena Vista in 1847. After the war, he was elected to two terms as a Whig in Congress, was appointed the United States minister to China and then returned home to serve two more terms as a congressman. When the Civil War began, Marshall hoped for Kentucky to remain neutral and stay out of the fight; however, when the state became a battleground in 1861, he accepted an appointment as a brigadier general in the Confederate army. In early December, he came through Pound Gap, a crossing point in the mountains between Virginia and Kentucky, with several thousand Confederate troops and occupied the Big Sandy Valley. His objectives were to hold the eastern part of the state, secure the loyalties of the people and recruit the locals to serve in the Confederate army.[71]

To place Marshall's and James Garfield's résumés side by side in December 1861, there was no question who was the more accomplished, experienced and by all measures better commander. When Marshall was fighting in Mexico, Garfield was leading mules on the canals of Ohio and attending small schools in the old Western Reserve. When Marshall was in China representing the United States, Garfield was graduating from Williams College in Massachusetts. Garfield had studied military manuals and tactics by candlelight as a state senator; Marshall had graduated from West Point in the same class as five other future Civil War generals. Despite these glaring differences, experience does not always dictate success or failure. For James Garfield, the campaign for the Big Sandy Valley would be a story of overcoming obstacles and succeeding in the face of adversity. Outnumbered, commanding inexperienced troops against a veteran officer, marching through the inhospitable mountains of eastern Kentucky and facing brutal cold and heavy snow, James Garfield and his command were to write their own chapter of the Civil War in the Big Sandy Valley in December 1861 and January 1862.

THE BIG SANDY VALLEY CAMPAIGN: "THE WORK WILL BE POSITIVELY ENORMOUS"

After the dramatic departure ceremony for the 42nd Ohio in Columbus, James Garfield arrived in Louisville, Kentucky, on the night of December 16, 1861. He was ordered to the city to meet with his new commanding officer, Don Carlos Buell. Frank Mason, a veteran and regimental historian of the 42nd Ohio, described Buell as a "cold, silent, austere man who asked a few direct questions, revealed nothing, and eyed the new comer with a curious, searching expression as though trying to look into the untried Colonel and divine whether he would succeed or fail." Determinations of success aside, Buell did not call Garfield to his headquarters in Louisville to provide him with detailed instructions for his upcoming campaign. Rather, he spoke with Garfield to apprise him of the situation in eastern Kentucky and to ask him what his plans would be to deal with Humphrey Marshall. Garfield was to design a plan for the campaign that evening and report to Buell in the morning.[72]

Garfield was surprised by such a daunting task. He had gone from training recruits to designing a specific campaign in an uninviting region against an unknown opponent in the span of just a few weeks. As he wrote years later, "It was a trying and unexpected responsibility to be placed on the shoulders of one who had never heard a hostile gun." With his task for the evening laid out, Garfield went to his hotel in Louisville and made his preparations. He spent the night studying terrain and troop movements, searching for the key to victory in the Big Sandy Valley. In many ways, his preparations for this campaign that evening resembled the countless nights he had spent through the years burning the midnight oil to study Latin, theology or algebra while a student and teacher at the Eclectic Institute in Hiram.[73]

At nine o'clock the next morning, as ordered, Colonel Garfield was present at Buell's headquarters with his plan for pushing Humphrey Marshall out of Kentucky. Despite his lack of experience, Garfield knew enough to realize that any military campaign relies primarily on supplies and logistics. Thus, in order to move into the Big Sandy Valley, he needed a means of supplying his men. The answer was in the name of the valley itself: the Big Sandy River. Garfield would operate along the river, using it to bring his supplies from the Ohio River to his men in the field. Using the river would allow Garfield's force to quickly advance on Marshall's position, one that the Confederates were able to hold only by long supply lines running over the mountainous terrain from Virginia. While presenting his plan to Buell,

Garfield was worried that it would not be well received, believing that "few officers in the service possess more reticence, terse logic, and severe habits of military discipline than General Buell." Through the conversation, Buell was stoic, commenting little on what was being said. When Garfield was finished, he was sent back to his hotel to await his official orders. When they arrived that night, it was clear that Garfield's plan was a success; the orders mirrored what he had presented to Buell that morning:

> *The brigade organized under your command is intended to operate against the Rebel force threatening, and indeed actually committing depredations in Kentucky through the valley of the Big Sandy.*
>
> *The actual force of the enemy from the best information I can gather does not probably exceed 2,000 or 3,000, though rumors place it as high as 7,000. You can better ascertain the true state of the case when you get on the ground.*
>
> *You are apprised of the position of the troops placed under your command. Go first to Lexington and Paris and place the 40th Ohio Regiment in such position as will best give a moral support to the people in the counties on the route to Prestonsburg and Piketon, and oppose any further advance of the enemy on that route.*
>
> *Then proceed with the least possible delay to the mouth of the Sandy and move with the force in that vicinity up that river and drive the enemy back, or cut him off.*
>
> *Having done that Piketon will be probably the best position for you to occupy to guard against further incursions.*
>
> *Artillery will be of but little if any service to you in that country. If the enemy have any it will encumber and weaken rather than strengthen them.*
>
> *Your supplies must necessarily be taken up the river and it ought to be done as soon as possible while the navigation is open. Purchase what you can in the country through which you will operate. Send your requisitions to these Head Quarters for funds and ordnance stores and to the Quartermaster and Commissary at Cincinnati for other supplies.*
>
> *The conversation I have had with you will suggest more details than can be given here. Report frequently and fully upon all matters concerning your command.*[74]

While Garfield was glad to have Buell's approval, one point of concern was the lack of artillery. Garfield desperately wanted to have several pieces with him in the field, believing they could make a difference in battle. Buell decided against artillery, believing it too difficult to move cannons in mountainous terrain in the winter. Thus, Garfield was to have only infantry and cavalry at his command.

For the campaign ahead, a new brigade was formed, with Garfield at its head. The 18th Brigade, Army of the Ohio, consisted of the 42nd Ohio, now led by Lieutenant Colonel Lionel Sheldon; the 40th Ohio, commanded by Colonel Jonathan Cranor; the 14th Kentucky, with Colonel Laban Moore at the helm; the 22nd Kentucky, led by Colonel Daniel Lindsey; and eight cavalry companies from Ohio and Kentucky. While most of this force was gathered near Catlettsburg, the 40th Ohio was in Paris, Kentucky, and was to march overland to the area of Paintsville, where it hoped to come in on the flank of the Confederates in the valley. Before Garfield left Louisville, he spoke briefly with Buell, who advised him to stay in communication throughout the upcoming campaign. Buell provided a few words of encouragement, telling him, "I shall hope to hear a good account of you."[75]

Garfield understood the task before him. Even for a

The Big Sandy Valley, Garfield's first theater of war from December 1861 to March 1862. *From* Battles and Leaders of the Civil War.

veteran officer, the campaign would be daunting. He bore out his feelings and worries over the upcoming campaign in a letter to Harry Rhodes, written while in Louisville on December 17:

> *The work will be positively enormous, for a large share of the Kentucky forces are as yet unarmed and undisciplined. It is a horrible country, fully as rough as Western Virginia and the General intimates that I cannot leave there before spring. He said (and I fully agree with him) that he would much have preferred to have me with him in the grand column, but yet he said I would have a much greater chance for distinction. The territory I am to command covers more than 6,000 square miles. I must go to studying geography.*[76]

On December 20, when Garfield left for the field, he wrote to Lucretia, outlining the task that lay ahead. He wasn't happy about leaving the 42nd Ohio but was optimistic about the possibilities of brigade command, admitting, "I hardly know how I shall like the change, though I think I shall like the additional inspiration of increased work." From Louisville, Garfield traveled to Paris, where he linked up with the 40th Ohio and issued orders for its movement into the Big Sandy Valley. Garfield would not have direct contact with the regiment for some time, but it was to play an important role in the campaign.[77]

A few days later, Garfield arrived upriver at Louisa, where he joined his command. When Garfield reached his men, he found that many of them had been or were scavenging from locals. Considering his twin goals of repulsing Confederates from the region and securing the loyalties of the people for the Union, Garfield could not let these infringements go. He lined up his men and lectured them on proper conduct in wartime:

> *Soldiers, we came to Kentucky to help her sons free her sacred soil from the feet of the rebel horde now lying just behind that mountain range. Tonight, we go to dislodge them. Show these Kentuckians, who are your comrades under one flag, that you did not come to rob and to steal, but came to indicate the true character of the American soldier, and hereafter I shall believe that I command a regiment of soldiers, and not a regiment of thieves.*

Private Owen Hopkins wrote that many in the 42nd Ohio agreed with Garfield that it was wrong to "confiscate rebel property" at that time; however, as the war progressed and the men became combat veterans, "we totally forgot the moral teachings of Colonel Garfield."[78]

From Louisa, the 18th Brigade continued up the river and made camp at George's Creek on the night of December 25. The following day, Garfield sent two dispatches to Buell with word of his progress. At this point, Garfield had roughly 1,400 effective soldiers between the 42nd Ohio and the 14th Kentucky. Marshall's force, he believed, was 2,500 strong and fortifying in the mountains eighteen miles to the south in Paintsville. The roads of the valley were "almost impassable." Garfield noted that it took four days to bring twenty-five nearly empty wagons a distance of twenty-eight miles. Making matters worse, Colonel Lindsey reported that the 22nd Kentucky was not yet fit for field service and thus had not yet joined the brigade. All this made for a very difficult situation for any brigade commander, let alone one with no prior experience. Indeed, Christmas Day 1861 was a stressful time for Garfield.[79]

For several days, Garfield remained at George's Creek, gathering supplies and preparing his men to continue their southward push into the mountains. On December 28, Garfield sent orders to the 40th Ohio, directing it to close in on Paintsville from the west; Garfield himself would lead the rest of the brigade down from George's Creek. He hoped to confront Marshall's force on two sides, crushing the Confederates and clearing them from the area. While a good plan, it was hampered by the poor state of the roads and the intermittent winter weather plaguing his men.

As the 18th Brigade began to move again, Private Hopkins recalled that many soldiers did not possess tents or adequate shelter. Several nights in early January brought sleet and knee-deep snow that pelted the men on guard watching out for Confederate pickets. The area into which the brigade was entering appeared to be another world for many of these northeast Ohio natives. Frank Mason described the character of the region as "primeval barbarism."[80]

From working with local citizens, Garfield soon learned that Marshall and his army were camped and fortifying three miles outside Paintsville. By January 4, Garfield was closing in on the town. In a note to Buell, he emphasized the poor condition of the roads and the men under his command. His companies of Ohio cavalry, led by Major William McLaughlin, lacked carbines to fight with and were thus operating with muskets from those too sick to fight in the 42nd Ohio. He closed with an appeal for artillery to be sent to him, noting that he intended to test Marshall's men in battle within the coming days.[81]

Upon approaching Paintsville, Garfield was faced with a dilemma of how to advance on Marshall's position. The Confederates had posted defenses along several roads leading into the town, and concentrating too much on

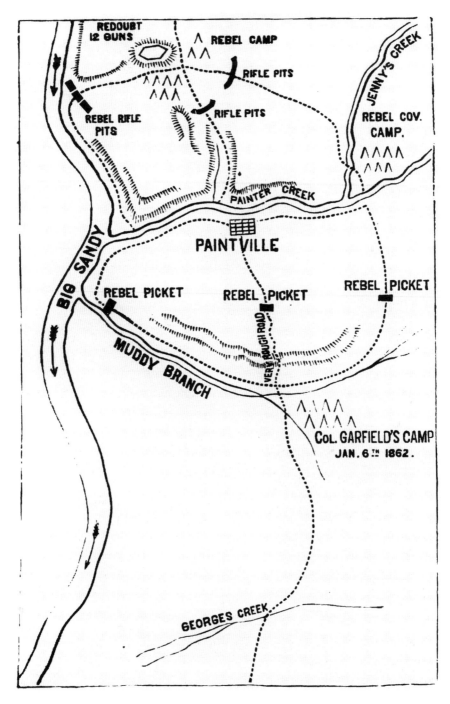

Garfield's maneuvers around Paintsville in early January 1862. *From James Brisbin's* The Life and Public Career of James A. Garfield.

any one path could lead to disaster for the Federals. How best to approach this town was to be Garfield's first tactical decision in the face of an enemy during the war. On January 5, Garfield made his first move against Marshall, one that proved to be more important than any casualty toll for the day might suggest. Despite the difficult terrain—Garfield described it as "the worst country to get around in I ever saw"—the 18th Brigade would undertake a fairly risky maneuver to try to force Marshall's Confederates out of Paintsville.[82]

There were three suitable approaches to the town, and Garfield decided to use all three. He began by pushing men along the river to extend the Federal left flank. Once Confederates responded to this threat, Garfield pushed ahead on a road on the far right of his position, forcing more Southerners to shift to Marshall's left flank. Once Marshall responded to the threat to his left, more Federals began moving toward Paintsville from the center of the Union line. Garfield was clearly taking a significant risk; he was dividing his command in the face of a numerically larger enemy force, using roads in poor conditions to threaten three points on Marshall's defensive line.

Despite this risk, there was also the opportunity for significant reward. These three advances, though small in number, were enough to project the strength of a significant Union force in front of the Confederates. The situation to his front, combined with intelligence that the 40th Ohio was closing in on his flank from the west, convinced Humphrey Marshall that there were over four thousand Federals threatening his line. Facing such odds, Marshall opted to abandon Paintsville and retreat southward. Garfield's gamble had paid off. On January 6, Garfield moved his command to the mouth of Muddy Branch to get supplies from the river, and on the following day, his men entered Paintsville. He sent a force of several hundred men after Marshall, but because of the cold and icy weather and deep mud on the roads, the column stopped and returned to Paintsville on January 8.[83]

As Marshall fell back, he first made his way to Hager Hill a few miles from Paintsville; from there, he moved farther south to Prestonburg. For Humphrey Marshall, the maneuvers around Paintsville had gone horribly wrong. While his command did not sustain any serious losses in manpower, it had lost an important defensive position along the Big Sandy River. This was yet another frustration in an already long and frustrating campaign. The weather, poor roads and terrain were as much a problem for Marshall's Confederates as they were for Garfield's Federals. Marshall's men were poorly supplied and appeared "more like the bipeds of pandemonium than beings of the earth," according to one citizen of the valley. One-third of the

Confederate force became ill and unfit for duty during the campaign. Not even the people of Kentucky offered any hope for Marshall's expedition; recruits from the civilian population were not nearly as plentiful as had been expected at the outset of the campaign. Marshall had a poor opinion of the locals in the Sandy Valley, describing them as "perfectly terrified or apparently apathetic." Because of the low rate of recruitment for his force, Marshall believed that many citizens sided with the Union but were "so ignorant they do not understand the question at issue."[84]

The retreat from Paintsville continued a downward spiral for Marshall's men. His force had started out the campaign with over three thousand men; now, with weather and disease ravaging his soldiers, Marshall had just shy of two thousand effectives left. On January 9, several of the officers in the 54th Virginia wrote a request to Marshall that the command pull out from eastern Kentucky so that it could rest and refit in winter quarters in the more hospitable and welcoming terrain of Virginia. "While we would be willing to make any sacrifice to advance our cause," the letter stated, "we felt satisfied that we can accomplish no good result this winter." Without proper reinforcements or supplies, the officers believed that the strength of the command would continue to fall.[85]

Marshall was not yet ready to abandon the campaign, however. He took up a new position a few miles outside Prestonburg, which was to offer better defensive terrain and the hope that finally, after weeks of marching through snow and mud with inadequate supplies and rations, something might go right for the Confederates. His force consisted of the 5th Kentucky, the 54th Virginia, the 29th Virginia, several artillery pieces and a battalion of cavalry. While they were tired, ragged and poorly supplied, Marshall's men still had two advantages that Garfield's troops did not: they were led by an experienced commander and they held good defensive terrain.[86]

While things were going poorly for Marshall, momentum was building for Garfield. He had advanced deep into the Big Sandy Valley, taken Paintsville and was now receiving some much-needed reinforcements. Several companies of cavalry arrived on loan for the 18th Brigade, courtesy of Garfield's close friend Brigadier General Jacob Cox, who was still in western Virginia at the time. Furthermore, on January 8, Colonel Cranor and the 40th Ohio finally arrived and linked up with Garfield's command. Having gone over one hundred miles across Kentucky to reach Paintsville, Cranor's men were exhausted and low on supplies, but at least they were there. Following his success at Paintsville, Garfield decided to gather supplies, distribute rations and use his reinforced brigade to make another push against Marshall's Confederates. He formed a force of 1,100 men from his four infantry regiments, as well as several hundred cavalrymen, to move south with him in pursuit of Marshall. Describing his plans to Buell, Garfield wrote, "I fear we shall not be able to catch the enemy in a 'stern chase,' but we shall try."[87]

The Battle of Middle Creek

Garfield set out from Paintsville on January 9 in pursuit of Humphrey Marshall, leaving behind a portion of his force to await further instructions. Garfield ordered five hundred of his cavalrymen to threaten Marshall's flanks, while his infantry was to advance directly on the Confederate position. They arrived at Abbott's Creek at 8:00 p.m. Garfield had closed in and was intent on fighting the following morning. Knowing that Marshall was near, he sent off an urgent dispatch to Lieutenant Colonel Lionel Sheldon in Paintsville, ordering him to bring up the rest of the 18th Brigade in support. "Get everything in good shape as possible, but *hurry, hurry, hurry*," Garfield urged. "Now or never we must strike them."

Garfield's men settled in on the cold Kentucky ground that evening. Without fires for warmth—they were forbidden due to the proximity to the enemy—many shivered and shook underneath what blankets and clothing they had. In Company F of the 42nd Ohio, Joseph Bowker recalled that his blanket froze to the ground that night, "making it difficult to get up the next morning."[88]

On January 10, Garfield did not let his men sleep for long, waking them before the rays of dawn broke through the frigid mountain air. Garfield believed Marshall's main force to be camped on Abbott's Creek. He intended to advance up Abbott's, cross over to the south and go upstream to Middle Creek, thereby getting behind Marshall and preventing him from escaping. This plan became obsolete when it was discovered that Marshall's men were in fact encamped a few miles up Middle Creek, which ran through steep ridges in the terrain. At 10:00 a.m., the movement of Ohio cavalry up the creek encountered mounted Confederates, and fierce skirmishing began. Garfield continued his progress, creeping closer to Marshall's main lines on the southern side of the creek. Marshall had posted his artillery, the 54th Virginia and a small reserve on his left, guarding his route of retreat, with the 29th Virginia and 5th Kentucky to their right covering the lower half of the ridge.[89]

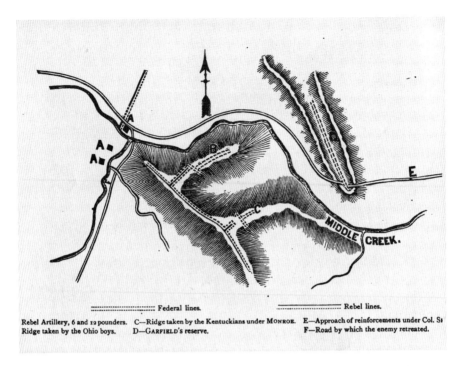

Federal lines. .... Rebel lines.

Rebel Artillery, 6 and 12 pounders.   C—Ridge taken by the Kentuckians under MONROE.   E—Approach of reinforcements under Col. St
Ridge taken by the Ohio boys.   D—GARFIELD's reserve.   F—Road by which the enemy retreated.

The Battle of Middle Creek, January 10, 1862. *From* Battles and Leaders of the Civil War.

By the time the Federals were ready to attack, it was noon. Unsure of the precise location of Marshall's lines, Garfield ordered twenty cavalrymen to dash across the valley, exposing themselves to the Confederates. When Confederate artillery fired at the mounted Federals, Garfield had a firm sense of where the enemy's guns were. He ordered his men to execute marching drills, allowing the Confederates to see some of his line but not all, obscuring how many were actually under his command. Soon after, he ordered his infantry forward. Companies A and F of the 42nd Ohio and Company A of the 40th Ohio crossed upstream to strike what they would soon discover were the lines of the 29th Virginia, while several companies of the 14th Kentucky were ordered to cross the creek slightly downstream and advance on the left flank of the Ohioans.[90]

Crossing Middle Creek, many of the men found the water to be waist deep, forcing the soldiers to hold their guns and cartridge boxes up to keep them dry. Once across, the soldiers attempted to "climb the almost inaccessible sides of the mountain, among rocks and briers, with scarcely a foot hold for 300 feet," as Private Bowker recalled. Private Hopkins noted that the climb was "almost perpendicular," and Confederate fire was incoming nearly the entire way. Once on top of the ridge, the Ohioans discovered that, rather than flanking Marshall's line as they were expecting, they were facing it head on.[91]

To the left, the 14th Kentucky was also having a difficult time. Watching from a hill on the opposite side of the creek known as Graveyard Point, Garfield sent in more men to assist the first wave of attackers. Major Don Pardee of the 42nd Ohio led several more companies from his regiment, as well as additional companies of the 14th Kentucky, across Middle Creek and up the opposite slope. Garfield described the subsequent fighting to Lucretia as taking place at extremely close range, so much so that "the combatants shouted and talked to each other while they fought."[92]

From the outset of the campaign, Garfield had continuously pleaded with Buell to have artillery with him in the field, believing it could make a difference in a fierce battle. Yet at Middle Creek, Marshall's artillery proved to be more of an encumbrance for the Southerners than anything else. Unfortunately for the Confederates, and much to the Federals' pleasure, the shells that were fired from Marshall's guns ended up being misfires or duds. Garfield related the story of a close call soon after he took position on Graveyard Point when an enemy shell landed in the ranks of one of the reserve companies. "The shell tore up the earth in the midst of the company," Garfield wrote, "but it did not explode. Had it done so, it would almost have annihilated the company." Marshall's men had hauled these heavy cannons over poor roads, up mountainsides and through the snow and sleet of the Kentucky winter for weeks. Now, when they were actually needed, they proved useless.[93]

Despite incoming fire, Garfield continued to manage the fight. He ordered Colonel Cranor's 40th Ohio to follow in the steps of Major Pardee's assault. While Pardee's men had struggled at first, the fresh help made a considerable difference, as Garfield himself noted. "Inch by inch, the enemy, with more than three times our number, were driven up the steep ridge nearest the creek." While Garfield's estimate of the Confederate strength was much too high, it was still a difficult uphill push for his soldiers. To the left of Cranor and Pardee, Garfield sent in the men of Colonel George Monroe's 22nd Kentucky to assist the 14th Kentucky in pressing against Marshall's right flank, held by the Confederate 5th Kentucky regiment. This part of the line was especially important to Garfield because it was laying down heavy musket fire on his command post at Graveyard Point. Garfield wrote, no doubt with some hyperbole, that "a thousand rifle balls came within a foot of me." Thus, Kentuckians who were loyal to the Union were advancing uphill against Kentuckians who were fighting for the Confederacy, all on the ridges surrounding Middle Creek in the remote eastern reaches of their home state. As the battle continued, "the hill trembled under the recoil," Garfield wrote.[94]

With nearly his full available force committed, Garfield could but wonder at the sights and sounds of his first significant combat of the Civil War:

> *The agony of the moment was terrible; the whole hill was enshrouded in such a volume of smoke as rolls from the mouth of a volcano, thousands of gun flashes leaped like lightning from the cloud. Every minute the fight grew hotter. I was just ordering my whole reserve in to line and was going to lead them up the hill myself when I looked and saw the Hiram banner sweep up the hill. I shouted to our boys to look. They saw, and such a shout of joy now greeted my ears.*

At this pivotal moment, with the battle still undecided, Lieutenant Colonel Sheldon finally arrived with the rest of the 18th Brigade from Paintsville. At 4:00 p.m., flying their regimental flag from Hiram, Sheldon and his nearly seven hundred men of the 42nd Ohio were sent right into the fight, following Cranor and Pardee up the slope and into the fray. The remaining companies of the 14th Kentucky were sent forward against Marshall's ineffective artillery, and now the full weight of the 18th Brigade was finally deployed against the Confederate line. With exhausted soldiers, many suffering from hunger and disease, these reinforcements were too much to bear for Marshall's command. By 5:00 p.m., the Confederates had fallen back from the mountain slopes and were in retreat.[95]

With darkness falling across the landscape, Garfield "deemed it unsafe" to continue his attacks, and the eventful day came to a close. That night, as Private Bowker recalled, the Confederates fell back from the field "by the light of their burning stores and camp equipage." Garfield wrote that the darkness was permeated by "a brilliant light streamed up from the valley… [Marshall] was burning his stores and fleeing in great disorder."[96]

The following day, rather than launch a pursuit of Marshall, Garfield withdrew his command to Prestonburg to the east. When he left Paintsville on January 9, Garfield's men had rations enough for only two or three days; any pursuit leading them away from their supply base was therefore impossible. Garfield hoped that Prestonburg would provide his exhausted but triumphant soldiers a source of rest and sustenance. He was sadly mistaken. "The place was almost deserted," he reported to Buell, forcing the 18th Brigade to fall back to Paintsville, where boats were still delivering supplies for the men. Rather than continue south to Piketon, as Buell had hoped, supplies forced Garfield to stay near Paintsville for the time being. He explained his withdrawal after the battle to Buell as one necessary because of logistics. "The marches over these exceedingly bad roads and the night exposures have been borne with great cheerfulness by my men, but they are greatly in need of rest and good care."[97]

The Battle of Middle Creek was over, and while neither side had been destroyed, each did claim victory in the days and weeks to come. Garfield believed that his men had killed 125 Confederates, wounding many more and capturing 25, all at a low cost to his brigade of only 3 dead and 20 wounded. When reporting the battle to Buell, Garfield stated that his army numbered only 900 engaged, while Marshall's command was 3,500 strong. In addition to the Confederate killed and wounded, Garfield's men seized over one thousand knapsacks and several hundred pairs of shoes, as well as Marshall's excess ammunition that was not burned.[98]

Marshall also claimed to have performed well at Middle Creek, telling his superiors that Garfield's attacks were slow and repulsed. According to Marshall, the Confederates lost only 11 killed and 15 wounded, while the Federals lost 250 killed and 300 wounded. "The field itself bears unerring testimony to his severe loss," Marshall surmised. He placed Garfield's strength at 5,000, as opposed to his own force of only 1,500. "I should have renewed the action after night," Marshall explained, "but an enemy greater than the Lincolnites (starvation) summoned me to reach a point where we might obtain food for man or horse." Marshall wrote that some in his command had not eaten for thirty hours before the battle, significantly weakening his already diminished force and making victory over the Federals nearly impossible.[99]

With such conflicting reports, understanding the specifics of what happened at Middle Creek is quite difficult. Some things about this fight, much like others throughout the war, will never be known. Totaling the exact strength of the combatants proves difficult, but by Marshall's own count, just days before the battle he had roughly 2,000 effective fighting men under his command. Garfield left Paintsville on the ninth with about 1,100 infantrymen and 500 cavalrymen, and when Sheldon arrived with the rest of the 42nd Ohio, another 700 troops were added to the total, giving the Federals upward of 2,000 men, though only the infantry was engaged in the fight. The casualty figures given by each commander were wildly inaccurate and completely typical of Civil War combat. The total casualties were under 100 for the day, not surprising given the inexperienced men, the relatively inaccurate muskets of each side and the difficult terrain over which the battle was fought.[100]

What is clear is that Middle Creek was a Union victory, and an indisputable one at that. Garfield had engaged Marshall in battle, driven him from the towns of the Big Sandy Valley and forced the Confederates to withdraw and flee farther south toward the Kentucky state line, accomplishing his primary objective for the campaign. Marshall attributed his retreat to a lack of supplies, as well as hunger and disease among his men, writing to Albert Sidney Johnston: "I am told by the commissaries that this country will be exhausted of all supplies in two or three weeks at furthest. What am I then to do?" Certainly, the difficulty of supplying his men and keeping them healthy was a dilemma for Marshall, but it was the presence of Garfield and his 18th Brigade that was the main reason for the Confederate retreat. Garfield had reclaimed the vast Big Sandy Valley and maneuvered Marshall out of his position at Paintsville, and when Marshall tried to hold firm defensive ground along Middle Creek, Garfield's soldiers had driven him back. While weather, supplies, disease and hunger all plagued Humphrey Marshall's campaign, none did so more than Colonel James Garfield and the 18th Brigade.[101]

One week after the fight at Middle Creek, Garfield issued a proclamation for his soldiers, praising their success in the face of great adversity:

Soldiers of the Eighteenth Brigade! I am proud of you all! In four weeks you have marched, some eighty, and some a hundred miles, over almost impassable roads. One night in four you have slept, often in the storm, with only a wintry sky above your heads. You have marched in the face of a foe of more than double your numbers, led on by chiefs who have won a national renown under the old flag, entrenched in hills of his own choosing, and strengthened by all the appliances of military art. With no experience but the consciousness of your own manhood, you have driven him from his strongholds, pursued his inglorious flight, and compelled him to meet in a battle. When forced to fight, he sought the shelter of rocks and hills. You drove him from his position, leaving scores of his bloody dead unburied. His artillery thundered against you, but you compelled him to flee by the light of his burning stores, and to leave even the banner of his rebellion behind him. I greet you as brave men; our common country will not forget you. She will not forget the sacred dead who fell beside you, nor those of your comrades who won scars of honor on the field. I have recalled you from the pursuit that you may regain vigor for still greater exertions. Let no one tarnish his well-earned honors by any act unworthy of an American soldier.

Remember your duties as American citizens, and sacredly respect the rights and property of those with whom you may come in contact. Let it not be said that good men dread the approach of an American army. Officers and soldiers, your duty has been nobly done. For this I thank you![102]

Written and issued in the immediate aftermath of battle, Garfield's proclamation certainly has its errors and flaws. They were not outnumbered two to one, and they did not kill nearly as many as Garfield believed. Such exaggerations based on misunderstandings were common right after a battle and would also come to be part of the acclaim given to the events at Middle Creek years later when Garfield's name entered into presidential politics. However, the majority of the proclamation deals in fact: the men were inexperienced, they were fighting against a veteran commander and they endured severe difficulties of weather and terrain. Despite all this, they had driven back Marshall's men.

Upon reaching Paintsville and allowing his men to rest, Garfield continued to revel in the glow of recent events. While the actions of his soldiers had dealt with the problem of Confederates in the Big Sandy Valley, he still needed to secure the loyalties of the local citizens. He issued a proclamation on January 16 for that purpose, telling them, in part:

I have come among you to restore the honor of the Union, and to bring back the old banner which you all once loved, but which by the machinations of evil men and by mutual misunderstandings have been dishonored among you. To those who are in arms against the Federal government I offer only the alternative of battle or unconditional surrender. But to those who have taken no part in this war, who are in no way aiding or abetting the enemies of the Union, but yet give no aid and comfort to its enemies—I offer the full protection of the Government, both in their persons and property.[103]

Just as they had different reports of the Battle of Middle Creek, the aftermath of the fight saw two opposite fates for Marshall and Garfield. For the obese Southerner, Middle Creek was the end of his advance into eastern Kentucky. He soon fell back twenty miles to the south, and within two weeks after the battle, Marshall was ordered to Pound Gap, where he had begun his campaign just two months before. Marshall had pleaded for reinforcements, going so far as to tell his superiors that unless he was reinforced, the chance of him successfully holding eastern Kentucky was nonexistent. No reinforcements were sent, and Marshall had to simply remain at Pound Gap for the time being.[104]

For Garfield, once news of the battle reached Ohio, it spread like wildfire, and friends, acquaintances and politicians began forwarding their congratulations. Just a few days after the battle, William Hazen sent his best wishes to Garfield, telling him, "I am delighted at your success in Eastern Kentucky. Nothing in the world has given me as much real gratification as this affair of yours with Marshall." On January 20, after receiving Garfield's reports of the action, General Buell extended his gratitude for the recent operations in the Big Sandy Valley. Overcoming difficult terrain, inclement weather and impassable roads and winning a battle without artillery were all credits to the remarkable skill and success of Garfield: "These services have called into action the highest qualities of a soldier—fortitude, perseverance, courage." From new Ohio governor David Tod—who had taken office just days before Middle Creek—came a dispatch regarding more supplies for Garfield's cavalry, as well as praise for the now thirty-year-old brigade commander: "We have all been greatly rejoiced at the success of Ohio troops under your command." Newspapers around the country spoke of the battle, including the *New York Times*, which celebrated the defeat of Marshall, whom it termed "the rotund rebel of Kentucky." With such effusive praise, many in Garfield's circle were beginning to talk of him receiving a brigadier general star. After the Battle of Middle Creek, things were clearly going well for Colonel James Garfield.[105]

In fact, Federal forces across Kentucky were having success in January 1862. Just as Marshall was pushing north into eastern Kentucky, Confederate general George Crittenden was coming north out of the Cumberland Gap, the main gateway to eastern Tennessee. Don Carlos Buell dispatched Brigadier General George Henry Thomas, a native Virginian who remained loyal to the Union, to deal with this threat. Thomas advanced southward and engaged part of Crittenden's command on January 19 at the Battle of Mill Springs, sending Confederates retreating south into Tennessee. Mill Springs was a slightly larger battle than Middle Creek, with a few hundred more casualties. The Union victory there catapulted Thomas to fame and is considered by many today as the first significant victory of the war for the North.

Just a few weeks later, on February 6, Brigadier General Ulysses S. Grant delivered an even larger and more impressive victory when he led a combined land and naval force that seized Fort Henry on the Tennessee River. Grant followed this up by moving east and forcing the surrender of over twelve thousand Confederates in Fort Donelson on the Cumberland River ten days later. Grant's demand for "unconditional surrender" at Fort Donelson echoed through the nation, making him an even larger hero than Garfield or Thomas. For now, it appeared as though Federals firmly held the state of Kentucky, and Ohioans had played a major role in the success. Forts Henry and Donelson had fallen to Grant, born in southern Ohio near Cincinnati in 1822; at Mill Springs, Thomas relied heavily on Colonel Robert Latimer McCook, a native of New Lisbon, Ohio. In eastern Kentucky, it had been a poor boy from the Western Reserve who became a college president, a state senator and then a Union army colonel who repulsed Humphrey Marshall.

While today few consider the action in the Big Sandy Valley when looking at the scope of the Civil War in early 1862, it was at the time considered in the same breath as the Union victories at Mill Springs and Forts Henry and Donelson. In late January, the State of Ohio passed a resolution thanking Colonels James Garfield and Robert McCook for their actions at Middle Creek and Mill Springs in driving Confederates from the soil of Kentucky, praising their "bravery in battle, and glorious victories over the enemies of the Union." Just a few weeks later, the Kentucky legislature followed suit, issuing its own resolution thanking Union officers and soldiers for freeing the state of Confederate troops:

The nation has been compelled by every patriotic motive to call upon her true sons to arrest rebellion, and preserve the government. Military men must put down rebellious politicians who have created the existing evils which threaten our destruction. Reason and entreats have failed, the sword is now to settle our destiny. While we fell sentiments of the highest admiration for all the brave officers and soldiers engaged in the cause of the Union wherever their field of operation may be, we entertain a particular gratitude to those who are driving our invaders from the soil of Kentucky. Therefore:
Resolved by the General Assembly of the commonwealth of Kentucky. That General Albin Schoeff, General William Nelson, General George H. Thomas, Colonel James A. Garfield, General U.S. Grant, and Commodore A.H. Foote, together with the brave officers and men in their respective commands, deserve the thanks of Kentucky, and the same are hereby most cordially tendered to every man of theirs for their brilliant victories achieved at Wild Cat, Ivy Mountain, Logan's Fields, Mill Spring, Prestonburg, Fort Henry, Fort Donelson.[106]

While the resolution referred to Middle Creek as Prestonburg, the meaning was the same. In the eyes of the Kentucky legislature, Garfield's efforts in the Big Sandy Valley during December 1861 and January 1862 were as important in saving the state from Confederates as other, more recognizable Union victories. Garfield's name was placed in between Thomas and Grant, men who would become two of the most famous generals of the war, and two men with whom Garfield would again cross paths later on in his life and career. Middle Creek had elevated the profile of a little-known former college professor and state senator from Ohio. James Garfield had inexperienced soldiers who were undersupplied in the dense forests, impassable roads and difficult winter conditions in the mountains of Kentucky, all while facing a commander infinitely more experienced in warfare than he. Despite these difficulties, Garfield had not only succeeded; he had triumphed in the face of adversity.

Middle Creek was by no means one of the largest battles of the war. Its small numbers and relatively low cost are such that it barely rates as a battle by most modern measurements. Its casualties were relatively few compared with the bloodshed soon to take place throughout the nation. Yet its impact was writ large on Kentucky and, in turn, the nation.

Pushing Marshall back secured the far left flank of the Union advance through Kentucky and into the western Confederacy. Garfield's actions

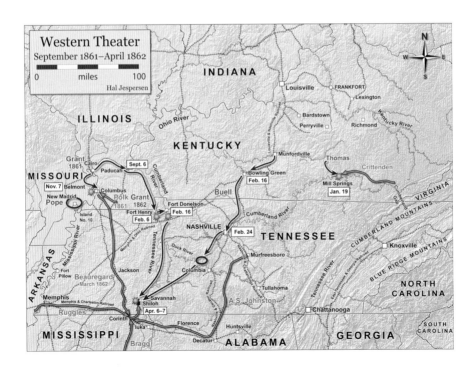

had an impact on not only the Big Sandy Valley but also Thomas at Mill Springs, Grant at Forts Henry and Donelson and the far right flank of the Federal advance, where Union troops would take Island Number Ten on the Mississippi in early April. These victories were like a wave sweeping through Kentucky and into Tennessee, cascading southward and gaining size, strength and significance as they pushed west. They broke through the vast front held by Confederates in the West and helped to secure an essential Border State for the Union. Certainly, Middle Creek was not on the same scale as the successes at Mill Springs and Forts Henry and Donelson. Grant's victories at Henry and Donelson opened up the Cumberland and Tennessee Rivers to Union forces, new avenues of advance that led to some of the most important gains of the war. The campaigns for Corinth, Chattanooga and even Vicksburg were all made possible by this success. Yet the Union advance through Kentucky needed to have the whole state clear of Confederates. Garfield's victory was an important part of that. In his history of the 42nd Ohio, Frank Mason expressed this same conclusion, noting that while his regiment went on to see action in larger and bloodier battles, "it may be fairly question[ed] whether the Regiment ever performed a day's duty of more timely and permanent value to the country…the victory at Middle Creek proved the first wave of a returning tide."[107]

Stretching hundreds of miles, Union forces were staging a massive advance southward in early 1862 that shattered the defensive lines that Albert Sidney Johnston had worked so hard to maintain. Kentucky was secure, at least for now, and the war would move south along the rivers and railways of the Confederacy.

CHAPTER 5

To Hunt Battles and Bloody Graves

I look upon the present, not only as the gloomiest hour of this war, but more gloomy than Washington's winter at Valley Forge.
—*James A. Garfield*

Having defeated Humphrey Marshall at Middle Creek, James Garfield had good reason to be pleased with himself in February 1862. Marshall's men had withdrawn back to Pound Gap, removing the main Confederate threat to the Big Sandy Valley. Despite this success, however, Garfield's task in eastern Kentucky was not done. Garfield was now faced with leading an occupying force and seeing to the administration of the area. He was responsible for the safety of the local population, keeping his men supplied and ensuring that Confederate troops stayed at Pound Gap. Though the Battle of Middle Creek was over, Garfield still had work to do in the Big Sandy Valley in the winter months of 1862.

Keeping his men supplied so deep into the eastern Kentucky mountains would have been problematic enough even in good weather. Garfield and his men would have to manage amid some of the worst conditions imaginable. Heavy rains came to the Big Sandy Valley, leaving the already abysmal roads and poorly supplied soldiers in worse shape than ever before. The situation was so problematic that on January 20, ten days after his victory at Middle Creek, Garfield requisitioned a steamboat and personally took part in an expedition up the Big Sandy to bring supplies from Cattlesburg to his men at Paintsville, Prestonburg and Piketon. The former canal worker was able to navigate strong currents, rocks, shoals and rains to successfully steer the ship and its supplies to his troops, in an episode that was remembered by many under his command for some time. On top of maintaining supply lines for his men, Garfield also spent the weeks of late January sending out cavalry and infantry patrols to drive away and even capture local bands of marauding Confederates and Southern sympathizers in the area.

While weather had been its foe for the entire campaign, it became a particularly difficult one for the 18th Brigade in late February. After the command had moved to Piketon, heavy rains caused the Big Sandy River to flood beyond its banks. This flood jeopardized the safety of both soldiers and the civilians of the valley, wiping out significant amounts of food and supplies that Union troops had painstakingly brought up the river. The rising waters swept away tents, shelters and even soldiers. Because the waters rose quickly at night, many were caught off guard by the sudden threat. Charles Henry, a soldier in the 42nd Ohio, recalled that the sunrise that morning "revealed the Big Sandy in all its fury." Private Hopkins recalled waking up with water inundating his tent, causing him to either flee or drown. Another private remembered floodwaters immersing the town and trapping part of Company F of the 42nd Ohio on a small island. The waters were so swift that the men of the 40th Ohio lost most of their tents and supplies without having a chance to recover them.[108]

Garfield wrote that the flood was more dangerous to his men than Humphrey Marshall's command had ever been, noting that for the first time in his military career, he was conquered. "In one hour the water rose twelve feet…The house where I am staying is sixty feet above the usual level of the river is now surrounded." Trying to salvage his command, Garfield rode through a strong current to check on the men of the 42nd Ohio, most of whom had given up their tents and shelters to local citizens whose homes were destroyed. With tents swept away and countless horses drowned, the flood was a disaster for the 18th Brigade. "I tremble for the sickness and suffering which will follow," Garfield wrote. "Four battles would not be so disastrous to us."[109]

Garfield was correct in his prediction of sickness sweeping through the camp. By early March, nearly five hundred men had been sent to the hospital because of disease. Along with the floods, the presence of soldiers in the region for the past several months had cleared it of extra food and supplies that could be beneficial to Garfield's command. In Company F of the 42nd Ohio, almost half of the men were sent to the hospital because of sickness. The spreading disease not only had an impact on the ranks of the

42nd Ohio but also left a mark on their commander. Garfield himself was afflicted by the effects of a smallpox inoculation in mid-February, which kept him confined to headquarters for over a week, though he was still issuing orders and going about his work. This was just the first of several instances when Garfield struggled with sickness during the war.[110]

Garfield bore his feelings in letters home to Lucretia, regretting the loss of the same young men he had recruited just a few months before:

> *I declare to you there are fathers and mothers in Ohio that I hardly know how I can ever endure to meet. A noble young man from Medina County died a few days ago. I enlisted him, but not till I had spent two hours in answering the objection of his father, who urged that he was too young to stand the exposure. He was the only child. I cannot feel myself to blame in the matter, but I assure you I would rather fight a battle than to meet his father.*

Garfield related a story where several men from the 42nd Ohio approached him in tears over their sickness and inability to recover. They feared death so far from home. He could do little but send them to the hospital for medicine and rest. "This fighting with disease is infinitely more horrible than battle," Garfield wrote. "This is the great price of saving the Union. My God, what a costly sacrifice!"[111]

Amid the difficulties of floods and illness, Garfield's passion for the war was not tempered. If anything, his first taste of combat had led him to believe all the more passionately that the war was a necessary undertaking to expand freedom in the United States. In February, he explained to a friend that the progress of the war was giving him "a few well defined conclusions…That this war will result fatally to slavery I have no doubt. This assurance to me is one of the brightest promises of the future." Few others at this time were so certain of the war's consequences, especially regarding the institution of slavery. Many in the North still believed that it would be possible for the conflict to end with slavery intact; indeed, many in the Confederacy hoped, prayed and fought for that end. In February 1862, the conflict was only still beginning in many ways, yet Garfield had a firm grasp of the issues at hand. He used his eloquence to lay out his feelings to Harry Rhodes:

> *Let the war be conducted for the Union till the whole nation shall be enthused, inspired, transfigured with the glory of that high purpose. Let all the deeds of valor add their glory of that high purpose, all the blood of noble*

men that die in the fight hallow it, all the love of the people for the fallen ones sanctify and exalt it, till the integrity, indivisibility, and glory of that Union shall gather round itself all the hero-worship, pride and power of the nation, and then, perhaps not till then, they will love the Union more than slavery and slay the python because its slimy folds roll toward the cradle of our infant Hercules (for the Union spirit is yet an infant compared with what it is to be.)[112]

Garfield knew that while things appeared to be going well for the Union at the moment, the war would not be over anytime soon. He noted to Lucretia that some believed the fighting would be done by June: "I, of course, am not so sanguine as to hope that."[113]

Garfield's success at Middle Creek brought great changes for the Union colonel. Most importantly, he was not to be a colonel much longer. Middle Creek provided the necessary battlefield success that his friends and allies in Ohio and Washington needed to put Garfield's name forward to the president for an appointment as a brigadier general of volunteers. On February 3, the Ohio Senate sent a signed statement to Washington asking President Lincoln to promote Garfield to the rank of brigadier general. All but two senators signed the measure, which stated that Garfield's "ability and skill as recently made manifest in Eastern Kentucky" more than justified such a promotion.[114]

Because of his connections in Columbus, many prominent Ohio Republicans were advocating on Garfield's behalf. William Bascom related this to Garfield, telling him that "all are pushing" to ensure his promotion. Among those assisting Garfield was none other than Lincoln's secretary of the treasury, Salmon Chase, a former governor of Ohio. Chase went so far as to note that Garfield received his promotion "at my insistence." With help from the Ohio legislature, Chase and others, the promotion went through, and James Garfield became a brigadier general in the Union army at the age of thirty. He received the news in March, but the commission was dated to January 10, the day of the Battle of Middle Creek.[115]

With promotions, floods and sickness, it would have been easy for Garfield to become too preoccupied to finish the job in eastern Kentucky. The Confederate threat still loomed, however; Humphrey Marshall's command remained near Pound Gap, and one more expedition was needed to push it out of the region for good. Confederate marauders had been harassing the local population, and as the Union commander of the area, it was up to Garfield to deal with the problem.

Brigadier General James A. Garfield, *Library of Congress*.

In mid-March, Garfield moved south with an expedition force of roughly seven hundred infantry and cavalry to confront the Confederate presence at Pound Gap, the entryway from Virginia into eastern Kentucky. Leaving Piketon on March 14, Garfield's men arrived at the gap and struck the Confederate force there two days later. The Federal cavalry advanced directly on the Confederate position, while the infantry advanced on the enemy from both the north and the south. After putting up a brief fight, the Confederates abandoned the position to Garfield's men. The Federals spent the night at the gap, made use of the abandoned Southern shelters and food stores and found correspondence from Humphrey Marshall regarding the poor condition of his command. Having cleared the Confederate threat for good, the force soon returned to Piketon, victorious once again.[116]

When Garfield arrived back in Piketon, his time in the Big Sandy Valley was coming to an end. With his promotion now official, new challenges, new commands and new battles beckoned. His record in the Big Sandy Valley over the past months had given his military career a tremendous start. Despite this success, the coming spring and summer would be difficult and frustrating times both for Garfield and the Union he was fighting to save. Soon, Garfield would trade the backwoods operations of Kentucky for an entirely new endeavor. Fittingly enough, the Disciple of Christ who had spent countless hours preaching in Ohio would see his first major battle of the war in the fields and woods surrounding a once peaceful church known as Shiloh.

THE BATTLE OF SHILOH: "THE BLOODIEST BATTLE EVER FOUGHT ON THIS CONTINENT"

While Garfield and his 18th Brigade were still in eastern Kentucky, the broad Union advance into the Confederacy was gaining steam farther to the west. After his victories at Forts Henry and Donelson in early February, now Major General Ulysses S. Grant began pushing up the Tennessee River and deep into the heart of the Confederacy. The target of this new Union offensive was the crucial rail town of Corinth, Mississippi, where the Memphis and Charleston and the Mobile and Ohio Railroads connected, linking together the Ohio River, the Gulf Coast, the Mississippi River and the Atlantic coast. For the Confederacy to successfully fend off Union thrusts into its territory in spite of its inferior manpower, shifting troops from one region to another was crucial, and railroads would be key to the effort. Union major general Henry Halleck, who was at the time commanding the newly created Department of the Mississippi, was overseeing the operation. Halleck's department included the commands of Grant and Don Carlos Buell's Army of the Ohio. Following the successes at Mill Springs and Fort Donelson, the pathway to Nashville had been opened up to Buell's army, and by late February, portions of the Army of the Ohio occupied the capital of Tennessee along the Cumberland River. With both Grant and Buell holding crucial rivers, Halleck's campaign to push into Tennessee came into focus. Grant's army would advance up the Tennessee River by gunboat, and Buell

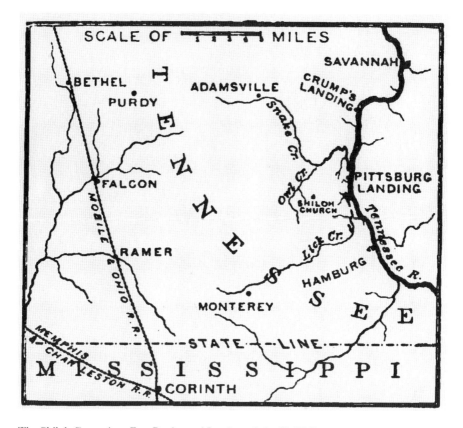

The Shiloh Campaign. *From* Battles and Leaders of the Civil War.

would move overland from Nashville to join him. Together, Grant and Buell would form a powerful striking force to damage Confederate infrastructure and reclaim vast portions of the western Confederacy.

By mid-March, Union forces from Grant's command began landing and disembarking from ships on the Tennessee River at a place known as Pittsburg Landing. By the end of the month, five divisions had made camp amid the plains, creeks and wooded lots of the landing, which became a launching point for a campaign southward.

This movement did not go unnoticed by the Confederates. With the Federal advances through Kentucky and into Tennessee, General Albert Sidney Johnston fell back deep into the South to regroup. Johnston went to Corinth to gather a broad concentration of Confederate forces to stop the Union advance. Named the Army of the Mississippi, Johnston and his second in command, P.G.T. Beauregard, worked together to form the disparate pieces into an army capable of stopping Grant's threat. By early April, there were over fifty thousand Confederates gathered at Corinth. Johnston knew that time was of the essence and that every passing day meant that Federals were gaining strength and posing an increasingly greater threat to the South.

This became even more apparent once Johnston received news of the imminent arrival of Don Carlos Buell and his Army of the Ohio. In mid-March, Buell began moving from Nashville. His destination was Pittsburg Landing, and soon, James Garfield would be joining him. In late March, once the operations around Pound Gap were complete, the 18th Brigade was broken up and Garfield and the 42nd Ohio were ordered to report to Louisville for a new assignment. Upon reaching Louisville, Garfield was told that he was to part ways with his beloved regiment. He was assigned the command of the 20th Brigade, 6th Division, Army of the Ohio, under the command of Brigadier General Thomas Wood, a man Garfield would come to know quite well through the course of the war. Wood was a native of Kentucky who graduated in the West Point class of 1845. He served in the Mexican War and was a longtime veteran of the U.S. Army when the Civil War began; he helped to raise and train troops from Indiana early on in the conflict.

Under Wood's command, Garfield was inheriting four regiments that were entirely new to him, only two of which were from his native state. The 64th and 65th Ohio Volunteer Infantries hailed from northern and northeastern Ohio; some of the men were even from Garfield's former senate district. Known as the Sherman brigade because of the recruiting influence of Garfield's fellow Ohioan, Senator John Sherman, these regiments would amass a remarkable combat record by the end of the war. Along with the two Ohio regiments, Garfield also had command of the 13th Michigan and 51st Indiana Volunteer Infantries.

Garfield was distraught at the thought of leaving the 42nd Ohio. He had been the first man in the regiment and raised many of its recruits himself through his passionate calls and speeches in Ohio. Garfield expressed his feelings in a letter to Frederick Augustus Williams, a member of the 42nd:

> *I would much prefer to have remained Colonel of the 42nd, than to have been promoted to any position away from them... The thought also of taking command of nearly 4,000 men* [a remarkable exaggeration on Garfield's part] *who had never been tried in battle, who were strangers to me and I did not know what officers I could rely on in an emergency made the future a gloomy one, especially as we were in immediate expectation of a great battle.*

The 42nd Ohio would go on to achieve fame on other battlefields of the war, as Lionel Sheldon and Don Pardee came to lead the regiment in their own right. The regiment gained notoriety for its honorable actions during the Vicksburg Campaign in 1863, and Garfield's own brother-in-law, Joe Rudolph, remained with the command through the rest of its service. Garfield maintained close connections with Sheldon, Pardee and the men for the rest of the war, always thinking of the regiment as his. While he left them in March 1862, his time leading the 42nd Ohio would always be a defining part of his Civil War service.[117]

Despite his regret at leaving, Garfield recognized that Buell had given him an opportunity for success in the army. The orders giving him a new command could not be ignored. He soon departed Louisville and made his way to Tennessee. He reached his new brigade on April 4, just as the men were making their way across the state for the grand campaign southward.

Thomas Tompkins of the 65th Ohio later provided a detailed account of the march across Tennessee to join Grant, noting the many difficulties that arose during the regiment's journey. "This was one of our hardest marches," Tompkins recalled, noting that the pace was "beyond the endurance of men." By the night of April 5, the men were nearing their destination but still had lots of marching ahead. During a moment of rest that evening, Tompkins laid on a bed of rails for an hour amidst a heavy rain that was drenching the brigade.[118]

Just as Garfield and his new command were marching to Pittsburg Landing, so, too, were Albert Sidney Johnston and his large Confederate force. Having received news of Buell's advance from Nashville, Johnston decided to attack Grant's men at the landing before their reinforcements arrived. On April 3, Johnston's army headed north from Corinth, battling the mud and rain of the southern spring to push toward their target. By the night of April 5, Confederates had come within striking distance of the mostly unsuspecting Federal camps at Pittsburg Landing. While several Confederate commanders believed that they had lost the element of surprise, thinking that surely the Federals knew of their presence, Johnston remained resolute, telling his commanders, "Gentleman, we shall attack at daylight tomorrow."[119]

The Battle of Shiloh began when Confederate forces swept upon the Union army in the pre-dawn hours of April 6, 1862, beginning the bloodiest combat ever seen on the continent up until that time. Over ten miles to the north, Ulysses S. Grant was still in Savannah, downriver from the battlefield. As Confederate brigades overran Union encampments, Grant was eating

The fighting at Shiloh was the bloodiest battle in American history at that time. *Library of Congress*.

his morning meal when the reverberating sounds of artillery caught his ear. Quickly, Grant made his way to his gunboat, the *Tigress*, and steamed upriver. He reached Pittsburg Landing by 9:00 a.m., disembarked and quickly began conferring with his commanders. Johnston's army had launched an attack with a broad front, striking several Union divisions and catching them almost entirely off guard. As Confederates drove into the Union lines, Federals gave way in an unsteady and chaotic fight. With the sounds of battle flooding the air, Grant realized that his army was being tested as never before. The key to the fight, as he told an aide, would be surviving until dark. Grant knew that reinforcements were on their way. If his Federals could last until help arrived, they could stem the Rebel tide and win the fight.[120]

In the coming hours, the Battle of Shiloh increased in ferocity and bloodshed. By mid-afternoon, Union forces had been driven back to a long defensive line running across the plains of Pittsburg Landing. At the center of the Union position, two divisions held an area known forever after as the Hornet's Nest. Here, Confederate troops launched numerous assaults aimed at breaking the Federal line. In the thick of the fighting, General Albert Sidney Johnston himself became a casualty, bleeding to death from a wound after leading a Confederate charge on the Union center.

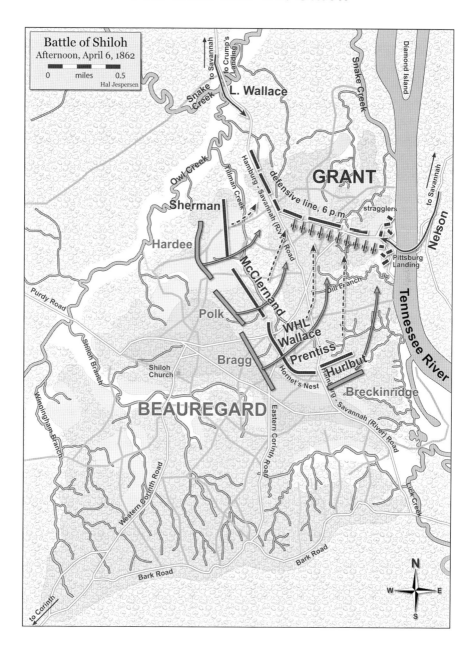

Throughout the day, as Federal units slowed the Southern advance, Grant was forming a new defensive position near Pittsburg Landing. The position utilized heavy artillery and the proximity to the landing to ensure that reinforcements and firepower would prevent the Federals from being swept into the river. By nightfall, Grant's army had fallen back to the refuge of this last line, repulsing several Confederate assaults before darkness finally brought an end to the day.

That night, rain fell across the landscape, covering the living, wounded and dying alike. Hogs rooted through the fields, feasting on the dead. Field hospitals were scenes of suffering, and the groans of the wounded still on the field were dissipated only by the rain and the darkness of night. Buell's army had begun reaching the field late in the day, and that evening, Grant's defensive lines were bolstered as reinforcements continued to arrive. For everything that had gone wrong that day, the Union army still had somehow held on.

As Garfield marched with his brigade on April 6, the sounds of battle from Pittsburg Landing echoed louder as they grew close. The men in the ranks were filthy from the long forced marches. During a halt for rest, Garfield rode along the ranks instructing the men to clean themselves up if possible. "We will give you some fun pretty soon," he was heard to exclaim. They marched through rain and darkness to reach the Tennessee River, where they arrived about 10:00 a.m. on April 7. At Savannah, Union gunboats were unloading the severely wounded before picking up fresh troops to send to the fight. While this was occurring, Garfield asked General Wood what his orders were for the division once it arrived. "Rush them onto the field," Wood instructed, "the work must be done." Soon enough, the division was moving south toward the sounds of battle.[121]

While Wood's division, including Garfield's brigade, was being sent upriver that morning, the fighting at Pittsburg Landing had resumed. Before 6:00 a.m., elements of both Grant's and Buell's armies began to advance and push back the Confederate battle line. By noon, Wood's division had finally arrived and disembarked at Pittsburg Landing. The Federal counterattack was in full swing at this hour, and Garfield and his brigade were sent to the front to take part. The men marched over fields and roads that provided ghastly sights, as Thomas Tompkins wrote: "The dead and dieing [sic] laid all around us here…A man was struck by shell, his stomach and insides fell at his feet. Oh if you like to see such sights, I do not." Garfield described the scene as "the most horrid carnage that any American battlefield ever presented."[122]

As Garfield and his men prepared to join the fight, General Beauregard, who assumed command of the Confederate army after Johnston's death, was faced with a decision. It was clear that thousands of Union reinforcements were pouring into Pittsburg Landing and turning to attack the Southern

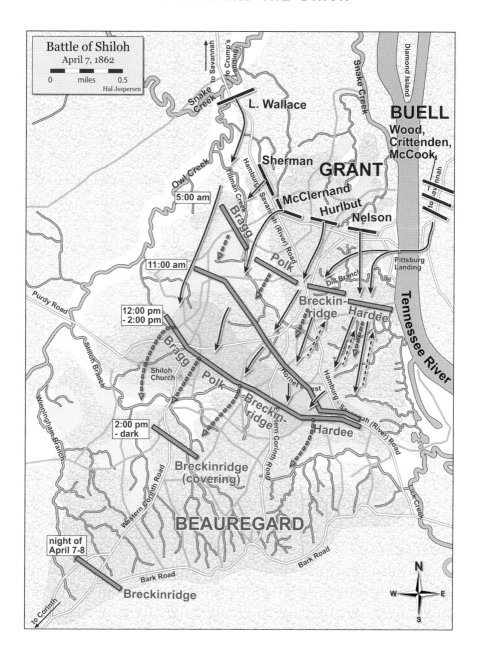

Battle of Shiloh
April 7, 1862

0   miles   0.5

Hal Jespersen

to Savannah

to Crump's Landing

Snake Creek

Diamond Island

L. Wallace

Snake Creek

BUELL

Wood,
Crittenden,
McCook

Sherman

GRANT

to Savannah

5:00 am

Owl Creek

Hamburg Savannah (River) Road

Tillman Creek

McClernand

Hurlbut

Bragg

Nelson

11:00 am

Polk

Pittsburg
Landing

Dill Branch

12:00 pm
- 2:00 pm

Purdy Road

Breckin-
ridge

Hardee

Tennessee River

Shiloh Branch

Bragg

Polk

Shiloh
Church

Hornet's Nest

Hamburg - Savannah (River) Road

Eastern Corinth Road

Breckin-
ridge

2:00 pm
- dark

Winningham Branch

Hardee

Breckinridge
(covering)

BEAUREGARD

Lick Creek

Western Corinth Road

night of
April 7-8

Bark Road

Bark Road

N
W   E
S

to Corinth

Breckinridge

lines. The element of surprise and numerical parity that had once been advantages to the Confederates were now completely gone. Despite having sacrificed so much, Beauregard believed he had no choice but to order a retreat. At 2:00 p.m., the orders to fall back were given.

By the time Garfield and his men reached the front, it was 3:00 p.m. His brigade halted at the cusp of the Union advance, and for a time the men were subjected to artillery fire. Garfield wrote that one of the shells narrowly missed him only to strike another officer nearby, turning the man and his horse into "a quivery mess of bleeding flesh." Despite the artillery fire, the 20th Brigade was not heavily engaged, and the Confederates were soon gone. Just as Garfield arrived, the Battle of Shiloh came to a close. The men spent the night at the front, and the following day they pushed forward in reconnaissance, only to encounter Confederate cavalry. In a sharp fight, the brigade suffered sixty-one casualties before it withdrew to the main Federal line.[123]

On April 6 and 7, 1862, over twenty-three thousand men were killed, wounded or missing at Shiloh. It was one of the great battles of the war. Others would soon eclipse it, but Shiloh stood as the bloodiest battle ever fought in American history at the time. Though fought in a remote wooded area on the Tennessee River, its impact would soon reverberate through the nation.

Despite Johnston's best efforts, Shiloh was a Union victory. Although Garfield did not see heavy combat, he and his brigade had still taken part. The arrival of the Army of the Ohio had been a major factor in the Union victory, helping to win the day on April 7. Historian Timothy Smith summarized the two-day battle accordingly: "If the first day put Grant in a position to win the battle, the second day's fighting would determine the extent of that victory." After Shiloh, Southern forces slipped back to Corinth to recover and defend the city as best they could. The loss of so many officers and men had been an irreparable setback, making it almost impossible for the Confederates to save the crucial rail junction. For the Federals, Grant had been caught off guard, but he recovered well and managed to turn a near disaster into a major victory. This was due in no small part to the timely arrival of Buell's command. Federal momentum in the West was slowed at Shiloh but certainly not broken.[124]

Ever since the battle, controversies have raged over generalship, bravery and the actions of various individuals. In a letter home on April 9, Garfield offered his own thoughts on Shiloh, writing, "On the whole this is no doubt the bloodiest battle ever fought on this continent, in which has been mingled on our side both the worst and the best of generalship, the most noble bravery and the most contemptible cowardice." He believed that Grant had been surprised, but the arrival of Buell's force turned the tide and stopped the Southern onslaught:

Dead horses at the Peach Orchard at Shiloh. The sights that greeted Garfield at Shiloh were ghastly and unforgettable. *Library of Congress.*

Inch by inch the enemy were driven back over the ground they had captured, and as night closed in, our line of battle, five miles in length, had swept the enemy back over a space of six miles. Such a scene as this 30 square miles presents beggars all attempt at description. If I live to meet you again, I will attempt to tell something of its horrors. God has been good to me and I am yet spared.

He closed the letter by providing directions for sending his mail, as well as reminding Lucretia, "Kiss our precious little Trot for me a hundred times. God bless you and her with the richest of his infinite love."[125]

THE SUMMER OF 1862: GARFIELD'S "VALLEY FORGE"

After the march to Pittsburg Landing, Garfield and his men were without their tents and camp equipment and would remain so for nearly two weeks. During that time, rain, exhaustion and sickness began to creep into the ranks. But there was to be no long respite from the war. The campaign for Corinth was on, and it was one of entrenchments and slow movements. After Shiloh, Henry Halleck arrived to personally direct the next stage of the Federal

Major General Henry Halleck. *Library of Congress.*

advance southward. Halleck's advance was slow and methodical, moving overland across the twenty miles between Pittsburg Landing and Corinth. Upon reaching the city, Halleck spread out his vast over 120,000-man army and laid siege to the Confederate positions, waiting for them to give up or withdraw, hoping to avoid a repeat of Shiloh's bloody casualty toll. Having arrived at the very end of the fighting at Shiloh, Garfield was anxious to take part in the action during the siege of Corinth. On May 28, Garfield lamented that fifty days had passed since the fighting at Shiloh, and still the Confederate army was not yet destroyed. "The fate of Corinth must soon be decided," Garfield wrote.[126]

While Halleck's maneuvering avoided massive casualties, it had the side effect of allowing the outnumbered Confederates to regroup in the city and plot their next move. Beauregard realized that holding Corinth in the face of such a force was unlikely; thus, he found a way out. By the end of May, Beauregard had abandoned the city. Federals had seized Corinth, but the Confederate army stationed there had slipped through their fingers.

The actions of the Corinth Campaign left an indelible impression on Garfield. When he first accepted his appointment from Governor Dennison in the 42nd Ohio, Garfield had requested that a West Point–educated officer lead the command; that was in the summer of 1861. Ten months later, by May 1862, Garfield had become disillusioned and fed up with professional military officers in the Union army, believing West Point–educated men were responsible for many of the ills plaguing the Union war effort. Garfield was frustrated that more had not been done to destroy the Confederate army at Corinth. While Union forces had captured the city, Garfield believed that a larger opportunity had been wasted. The manner in which the campaign

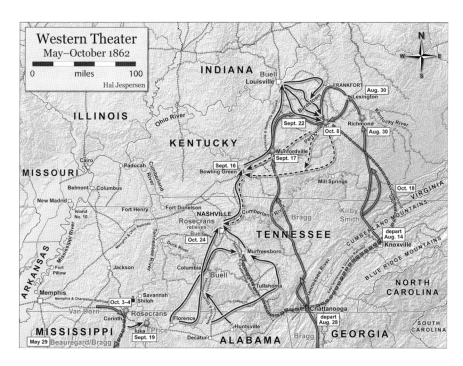

was conducted left him "disheartened," as he wrote to a friend in the 42nd Ohio: "There seems to be neither Generalship nor patriotism at the heads of the armies."[127]

While Garfield was frustrated at missed opportunities, he was even more incensed in his belief that regular army officers were trying to win the war while leaving slavery alone. Among them was none other than his division commander, Thomas Wood, whom Garfield described as "a very narrow, impetuous, proslavery man in whose prudence, and patriotism and brains I have but very little confidence." As the war progressed, Garfield's already strong views on slavery and abolition were only further cemented by his experiences in the field. His letters made numerous mentions of the apathy of other officers in the army to matters of slavery and freedom. Writing to Harry Rhodes, Garfield displayed his characteristic passion, alluding to slavery as a demon possessing both the nation and those who stood opposed to its abolition. "Before God I here second my conviction that the spirit of slavery is the soul of this rebellion, and the incarnate devil which must be cast out before we can trust in any peace as lasting and secure. It may be a part of God's plan to lengthen out this war till our whole army has been sufficiently outraged by the haughty tyranny of proslavery officers and the spirit of slavery and slaveholders."[128]

Garfield's frustrations over slavery, the prosecution of the war and West Point army officers were not unique to him. The same questions affected the highest levels of the Union army and the Lincoln administration, playing out on the grand stage of the war throughout its duration. In fact, later in 1862, Garfield was to play a prominent role in one of the most highly politicized chapters in the struggle between radical Republicans and the West Point conservatives.

After the fall of Corinth, Garfield and his command were sent to Iuka, Mississippi, for a new assignment. Thomas Wood's division was shifted from active campaigning to working on railroads in the area. The men began moving east, slowly working on and fixing parts of the Memphis and Charleston Railroad, making their way toward Decatur, Alabama. This slow pace bothered Garfield, who longed for battle once again. With their eastward trajectory, the brigade appeared headed toward Chattanooga and eastern Tennessee, though Garfield was unsure if that meant a return to combat.[129]

With slow service and the heat of summer, a long lingering health issue reared its ugly head for Garfield. He was afflicted with severe bouts of diarrhea and digestive troubles, slowly sapping his strength. In the span of just a few months, Garfield lost over forty pounds from loss of fluids and poor nutrition. He began to worry that his sickness would not subside but instead linger and become a chronic condition. In early June, a surgeon on his brigade staff recommended that he go home on a thirty-day leave, but Garfield preferred to stay with his men for the time being. Certainly, his physical problems did not ease his burdens of command or his irritations at the course of the war.[130]

Illness was not the only thing wearing on Garfield that summer. As his command was moving eastward, he was assigned to court-martial duty not once but twice. The first trial was for a lieutenant in the 58th Indiana, which occurred in June. In early July, he sat on a second court hearing for the case of Colonel John Turchin, who was charged with taking out his frustrations on the town of Athens, Alabama, tearing it apart and destroying civilian property. Throughout the trial, Garfield's position on the actions changed from disapproval to acceptance. The Turchin court-martial further helped to cement Garfield's growing indignation with the soft-handed prosecution of the war. He believed that more care was exerted to protect Southern civilians and Confederate property than was being exerted to assist slaves in the Southern states. "Until the rebels are made to feel that rebellion is a crime which the government will punish there is no hope of destroying it," he lamented.[131]

On a larger scale, Garfield's malaise was typical for the Union cause in the summer of 1862. After the victories of the year's early months, Union momentum had ground to a halt. Halleck's force spread out from Corinth, but no major battles occurred. In the East, Major General George B. McClellan led his grand Army of the Potomac to the Virginia Peninsula in an attempt to capture Richmond and win the war. After weeks of slow movements, Confederates stopped McClellan's advance in early June, and after the Seven Days' Battles of late June and early July, McClellan's Federals fell back toward the James River, relinquishing ground to Confederates led by Robert E. Lee. On top of these setbacks, rumors were rampant that England and France were on the verge of recognizing the Confederacy. Despite the success that occurred in early 1862, the Union war effort had hit a low point that summer.

Garfield poured out his feelings regarding these events in a letter to Captain David Swaim, an officer in the 65th Ohio whom Garfield had chosen to work on his brigade staff. Garfield and Swaim developed a close friendship in 1862 that would last until the future president's death nineteen years later. In a letter to Swaim, Garfield made clear the despair and frustration that had overtaken his vision of the war: "I look upon the present, not only as the gloomiest hour of this war, but more gloomy than Washington's winter at Valley Forge." Garfield elaborated by listing the failure of the Peninsula Campaign, Halleck's lackluster effort in the West and the looming specter of foreign intervention as reasons for such pessimism. "An overwhelming blow, bloody and soon, is all that can save us," he continued, adding that "it may be necessary to scourge us to that extent before we shall be willing to use all our own strength, by striking the enemy's weakness." Gripped by such doubt, Garfield believed the only recourse was to prepare for the struggle ahead: "Bid farewell to our dreams of peace and home. Our wisest work will be to hunt battles and bloody graves. But let us hope there is light behind this cloud, or else that the cloud exists only in my imagination."[132]

With frustrations mounting and sickness increasingly ravaging his body, Garfield would not remain in the South much longer. During the Turchin court-martial, illness had weakened Garfield to such an extent that he had difficulty sitting upright on occasion. By late July, a special order was issued to relieve him of his brigade command and allow him to go on sick leave. His sickness was just the last in a series of disappointing events that summer. From the highs of Middle Creek, Garfield had seen the worst of what the war had to offer. He left the men of the 42nd Ohio, he witnessed the bloodshed and slaughter at Shiloh, he was increasingly disillusioned with West Pointers and their soft-handed approach to the war and he was beset by illness so severe that he was forced to temporarily leave the army. In this regard, his personal struggles mirrored the larger troubles plaguing the Union at that time. Just as Garfield compared the challenges facing the Union war effort in July 1862 to those facing Washington's Continental army at Valley Forge in the winter of 1777–78, he himself was going through his own personal Valley Forge. Together, these disappointments formed the low point of the war for Garfield, but his return home to Ohio would provide rejuvenation and a rebirth for his political and military career, one that would take him to the very heart of the Union war effort: Washington, D.C.

CHAPTER 6
The Politics of War

AUGUST 1862–JANUARY 1863

So I shall try the rough sea—if the bullets will let me.
—James A. Garfield

When Brigadier General James Garfield arrived home in Ohio, he was a man beaten down by frustration and illness. Among the first events of his homecoming was an official examination to determine just how sick he actually was. On August 4, the Official Board of Surgeons, convened at Camp Chase in Columbus, provided an official statement and recommendation on Garfield and his continued service in the army. The board found him "suffering from a slight fever, loss of appetite, diarrhea, great muscular exhaustion, and excessively jaundiced." The James Garfield who appeared in Columbus in early August 1862 was a shell of the man who had worked there one year before to recruit the men of the 42nd Ohio. The recommendation of the board was for Garfield to stay home and rest: "The General will not be able to resume his duties in a shorter time than thirty days from this date."[133]

The illness Garfield was facing was akin to the enemy on the battlefield. For months he had been waging a war of attrition against it; now, he tried retreat. When he finally arrived in northeast Ohio, Garfield was at first overwhelmed by friends, well-wishers and political acquaintances, all wanting his time and attention. In such an environment, his recovery would be an uphill struggle. Because of this, in mid-August, Garfield, Lucretia and their young daughter, Eliza, retreated to a cabin in Howland Springs. The cabin was away from friends and well-wishers, allowing him the chance to recover and spend time with his family. He described it as "a quiet farmer's house shut up in the woods on a hill."

Years of political campaigns, preaching on the circuit, lecturing around the state and now fighting a war meant that James and Lucretia had spent a considerable amount of time apart during their still young marriage. For years, their relationship was strained by professional responsibilities and a lack of personal passion. Yet their secluded retreat in August served as an occasion for James to regain not only his physical health but his marital happiness as well. As Garfield rested and spent time with his wife and child, his recovery began. He was removed from the rigors and responsibilities of being a general, and being in Ohio with his family was a tonic for his illness. Writing to Lucretia several weeks later, Garfield expressed gratitude for the time the two had spent together, referring to it as a "baptism into a new life…I bless our Good All Father who has brought us through it all and I trust our love will be all the more perfect, being made so through suffering."[134]

On September 2, Garfield wrote to tell his mother of his improved condition. He told her their cabin was "a very pleasant place" that did much to aid his recovery. His weight had steadied, and the jaundice was leaving his skin. Altogether, he was doing quite well. Garfield's recovery was coming at a good time for him. While he recuperated, events were occurring within the Nineteenth Congressional District that would have a major impact on his personal and professional future. He was about to be nominated to run for Congress.[135]

The effort to nominate Garfield began before he arrived home in Ohio on sick leave. Even in June, Garfield was asked about his feelings on running for Congress, to which he responded favorably, stating that, with the way things were progressing at the time, he preferred "a seat in Congress to any place in the army or indeed to any place which West Point management will be likely to assign me." Garfield was a brigadier general with political experience and was widely respected within the state. Thus, he was a perfect match for the Nineteenth Congressional District. The district had previously been represented by the abolitionist firebrand Joshua Giddings, and many saw Garfield as cut from the same cloth. Though not quite as strong an abolitionist as Giddings, Garfield was willing to fight for his convictions in the field. His friends and supporters back home—including his frequent correspondents Rhodes and Hinsdale—went about garnering support and writing letters praising Garfield, all while he was hundreds of miles away in the Deep South that summer.[136]

When he returned home in August, the momentum for his candidacy had grown, posing a serious question for the general: if he were nominated, would he resign his commission to serve in Congress? On August 12, Hinsdale wrote to ask Garfield about the nomination, and three days later, Rhodes did the same. "I have no doubt that you will be nominated if you consent to run," Rhodes told Garfield, adding that if he were to be elected, it would mean the end of his military career because he could not be a sitting congressman and serve in the field simultaneously. Garfield acknowledged this reality in a letter to Hinsdale in which he provided his official intentions to his supporters. If he were to be elected, he would resign his commission, although he preferred to remain on active duty up until the time he took his seat. This decision meant that even if Garfield were elected in the fall of 1862, he could still have another year in the army because the next congressional session would not begin until late 1863. While stating his position regarding Congress and the army, Garfield expressed that he did not want to personally seek the nomination: "I should consent to accept it only on the grounds of displeasing the spontaneous wishes of my fellow citizens."[137]

The Republican nominating convention for the Nineteenth District met on September 2. Garfield was not present but still recuperating with Lucretia in Howland Springs. Several rounds of balloting occurred, with Garfield competing well against incumbent congressman John Hutchins. Garfield won the nomination on the eighth ballot, becoming a Republican candidate for Congress.[138]

With a nomination to run for Congress in hand, September saw a return to prominence for Garfield. He had escaped mundane railroad duty in the Deep South, he survived his serious health issues, he rekindled his marriage and his love for Lucretia and he had a possible seat in Congress ahead of him. Yet Garfield was still anxious to return to the war. The summer of 1862 was a desperate one for Federal forces across the map. After stopping George McClellan's push on Richmond in the Peninsula Campaign, Confederate general Robert E. Lee moved into Northern Virginia and handily defeated Union forces under General John Pope at Second Manassas in late August. That same month, Confederate general Braxton Bragg led Southern troops northward into the state of Kentucky, threatening the crucial Border State once again. In early September, Bragg's northward push was echoed by Lee, who took his Army of Northern Virginia into the state of Maryland. A broad Confederate front was threatening the Union with defeat. In the midst of these grim circumstances, Garfield left Ohio on September 16, journeying to Washington, D.C., to see what he could do to help his country in its hour of need.

On the eve of his departure for the East, Garfield laid out his thoughts on the recent events of the war to Burke Aaron Hinsdale, stating of the times: "The war is now strangely mixed, and the days are sufficiently dark." He spoke of his rest and recovery, noting that he was "freed from active cause of disease" and that he had already begun regaining the weight his illness had cost him. The pounds he lost were nearly all muscle, and thus it would take him time to recover his strength. He was not yet ready for service in the field. While he expressed a desire to command a division of troops, he readily admitted he had no notion of where his next command would come. Since he had last been in the field, Garfield's distrust of West Pointers had not waned. The professional army officers "have no confidence in each other—nor the people in them," he lamented. Garfield worried that the Confederacy would soon gain European recognition, all but ending the war and the Union. Only the subjugation of the South would lead to an end to the conflict. "We can never hope for peace till we crush up or disperse their heavy armies—and remove the active cause of the sectional feud."

In regard to his political future, Garfield was not as optimistic as could be expected. With his characteristic humility, Garfield eschewed his own ambitions, stating that he was proud of not having sought the congressional nomination for himself. While he preferred to remain in the quiet of private life, where he felt he would most benefit from "private study," he would continue on his path of public service if called upon. He was weary of the coming years, however, believing they would "be as fatal to political longevity as the war is to personal life and health." Garfield was wise enough to realize that the continuance of the war posed major problems for Congress and the nation. Such concerns aside, Garfield was determined to continue fighting for the country's future. "I would not, however, wish to be cowardly and shirk the responsibility of thinking and acting because the times are dangerous," he wrote. "So I shall try the rough sea—if the bullets will let me."[139]

"LIGHT IN THE MIDST OF DARKNESS"

James Garfield arrived in Washington on the morning of Friday, September 19, 1862, in the midst of one of the most momentous months in American history. Two days before his arrival, Union and Confederate forces had squared off at the Battle of Antietam in western Maryland; the sanguinary battle there saw over twenty-three thousand casualties in one day, the bloodiest single-day battle in all of American history before or since. When the guns fell silent, Robert E. Lee withdrew back into Virginia, and George McClellan held his army in Maryland, having repulsed the Confederate threat. Antietam would dictate the future course of the war in many ways. Not only was the conflict to become bloodier and more savage, but it was also to take on entirely new consequences in the battle's immediate aftermath. In July 1862, Lincoln had informed his cabinet that he was intent on issuing an emancipation proclamation that would free the slaves in the Southern states in rebellion. Based on the advice of Secretary of State William Seward, Lincoln decided to wait for a Union victory before issuing his proclamation. Two months later, once it was clear that the Confederate Army of Northern Virginia had left Maryland after the bloodshed of Antietam, Lincoln had his victory.

Three days after Garfield's arrival in Washington, on Monday, September 22, 1862, Lincoln announced to his cabinet that he was issuing the Preliminary Emancipation Proclamation. It was a military measure declaring that, under Lincoln's constitutional authority as commander-in-chief, slaves in the Confederate states actively fighting the government would be freed. It gave the Confederacy one hundred days to give up the fight—something that no one expected it to do—before the document would take effect. When the final version was signed on January 1, 1863, Lincoln declared all slaves in the states in rebellion to be forever free. It was a dramatic and powerful measure, infusing new life and purpose into the Union war effort. The war for the Union would now be a war for a better Union, one without slavery.

As a war measure, Garfield had hoped for an emancipation proclamation for many months. He long believed that slavery was the centerpiece of the Confederacy and the primary cause of the war. Garfield saw the destruction of slavery as the only guaranteed way to win the war and crush the rebellion. However, despite his hatred of slavery, when some radical Republicans were calling for the president to declare an immediate abolition of slavery early on in the war, Garfield believed the timing was not right. Writing in February 1862, Garfield stated his belief "[t]hat this war will result fatally to slavery I have no doubt. This assurance is to me one of the brightest promise[s] of the future. But I am equally clear that a declaration of emancipation by the administration would be a most fatal mistake…Nothing but the terrible logic of events will do it. That logic is at work and will surely do its work, but not yet."[140]

Once Lincoln issued the preliminary proclamation, however, Garfield realized that the time had come to advance the cause of freedom and bring about the abolition of slavery. "I am rejoiced at the President's proclamation," he wrote. "It gives us light in the midst of the darkness and shows us the beginning of the end. The people will hail it with great joy."[141]

Upon arriving in Washington, Garfield first took up residence at the famed Willard Hotel, the same hotel where Lincoln stayed before his inauguration in 1861. Because Garfield was a young and rising Republican and a Union general, the Willard would not remain his residence for long. Within a week, he received an offer from Secretary of the Treasury Salmon

Secretary of the Treasury Salmon P. Chase. *Library of Congress.*

Chase and his daughter Kate to stay with them at their home in the city for as long as he was in the capital. As a former governor of Ohio who had worked to ensure Garfield's promotion early in 1862, it was fitting that Chase took Garfield into his home. Through Chase and his daughter Kate, Garfield became acquainted with many high-ranking Republicans and administration officials in Washington, becoming very well connected. Indeed, under Chase's guidance, Garfield's political star continued to rise during his time in the capital.

While Garfield was well connected in Washington, he was acutely aware that the war was still going on, and it was doing so without him. He sought a military command, but none materialized. Certainly, there were many opportunities. Garfield's name was mentioned for commands in Florida and South Carolina. Yet in each case, something came up preventing the move. His letters mentioned frustrations, telling Lucretia, "You can understand without my saying how keenly I feel this delay and how it makes me feel that I am not doing the service any good." Making his wait in Washington worse was his already deep dislike and distrust of West Point officers. He hoped to avoid serving under someone like George McClellan, a moderate who in the eyes of many Republicans failed to grasp the severity of the rebellion, preferring to use a softer approach in waging war. Of all the West Point generals who angered Garfield, perhaps none did so more than McClellan. Garfield filled his letters with scathing indictments of the general, criticizing his conduct during the Second Manassas campaign, as well as his perceived failures at Antietam in September. In one particularly fiery passage, Garfield predicted that McClellan and his like would lead to the end of the nation, something he did not wish to live to see:

> If the Republic goes down in blood and ruin, let its obituary be written thus: "Died of West Point." Unless help comes soon, that ignominious death will stare us in the face. For myself, I say in all sincerity I have no wish to survive this republic, and if the end must come I hope I may find a bed like Kearny's.[142] I am passing through a terrible ordeal of personal suffering over the whole matter. I cannot believe I shall be kept here much longer.

Garfield sought a return to combat, but his wish would have to wait for several months still. While his time in Washington would eventually lead to another post in the field, Brigadier General James Garfield's next battle was not to be one against Confederates but a political fight within the confines of the capital.[143]

THE FITZ JOHN PORTER TRIAL

Before Garfield had arrived in Washington, events were transpiring on the fields of Virginia that would soon impact his life. At the Battle of Second Manassas in late August, Major General John Pope's Army of Virginia sustained one of the worst defeats suffered by any Union army during the war at the hands of Robert E. Lee and the Confederate Army of Northern Virginia. Pope had assumed his command earlier that summer while promising to give no quarter to the enemy and to bring a bold hand to the war in the East. He rose to prominence through success in the West, and the Lincoln administration hoped that bringing him to Virginia would provide a dramatic change of pace from McClellan's passive approach to the war. Pope's crushing defeat at Second Manassas put an end to those hopes, and McClellan was soon back in charge at Antietam in September. Pope was angered at his misfortune, and in the politically charged climate of the late summer of 1862, he looked for someone on whom to focus the entirety of the blame for his battlefield defeat. His blame and scorn were quickly placed on McClellan's closest friend and ally in the East.

Major General Fitz John Porter was an accomplished officer by August 1862. A member of the West Point class of 1845, Porter was a Mexican War veteran who began the Civil War as a Union staff officer in the regular army. He had a close friendship with George McClellan that only grew stronger as the war progressed, and the rise of McClellan enabled Porter's own ascension through the ranks. By the fall of 1861, when McClellan was made general-in-chief, Porter was a division commander in the Union army. A quiet and reserved man, Porter was a conservative who opposed radical Republicans and their attempts to transform the war into one for the abolition of slavery. This made him the opposite of many non–West Point officers in the Union army, James Garfield among them. During the Peninsula Campaign, Porter was given command of the Federal Fifth Corps, a position that he held under Pope during the Second Manassas Campaign.

Porter strongly disliked Pope both personally and professionally. He wrote several letters that were highly critical of the general and his leadership, expressing considerable regret that McClellan was not in charge of the Union offensives in Virginia. These letters eventually found their way into the hands of the Lincoln administration and subsequently into the hands of John Pope. As a result, animosity existed between Porter and Pope, a bad mix for commanders leading troops into battle.[144]

This sour relationship hit an especially low note of discord during the fighting at Second Manassas. On August 29, Pope ordered Porter to strike the right flank of the Confederate position as well as to stay in contact with the division of Major General John Reynolds. These two objectives were contradictory and made the orders difficult to follow. Accordingly, when Pope's orders to Porter were delivered late in the day, no attack was launched. Porter had intelligence that Confederates under James Longstreet were arriving in force on his flank, which further complicated the matter. He passed the intelligence on to Pope, who did nothing with it. Considering his confusing orders and intelligence of a Confederate threat to his flank, Porter was wise in

Major General Fitz John Porter. *Library of Congress.*

erring on the side of caution. Pope did not see things his way, however, and was furious that Porter did not move forward as ordered. On August 30, Pope again ordered Porter to attack. When Porter obliged and attacked along with the bulk of Pope's force, a large Confederate counterattack swept into his flank and ultimately routed the Federals from the field at great cost.[145]

The days following the disaster at Manassas were full of recriminations, and few were immune from the blame. George McClellan, John Pope and Irvin McDowell all fell under great public scrutiny. While many blamed John Pope for the disaster that befell his army, Pope himself turned his anger on Fitz John Porter. Ever since Pope had become aware of Porter's criticisms of him and his command, he had been skeptical of the Fifth Corps commander. Porter's actions on August 29—failing to attack despite Pope's direct orders— were the final straw. The first days of September saw George McClellan put back in command of all forces in and around Washington, effectively ending Pope's tenure in the eastern theater of the war. Pope was soon sent west to Minnesota to take command of the new Department of the Northwest, in effect a military exile. Before Pope left, he provided Lincoln with a scathing report charging Fitz John Porter, along with Generals William Franklin and Charles Griffin, with insubordination. A court of inquiry was ordered for all three commanders, and Pope was soon gone.[146]

With the Antietam Campaign in September, charges would have to wait. Porter once again commanded the Fifth Corps in the field. After Antietam, McClellan stayed in Maryland for nearly two months, much too long a period for Lincoln, who removed McClellan from command on November 7, 1862. With McClellan gone, Porter was relieved of his command three days later, on November 10. Soon, a commission was held to determine charges on Porter's conduct at Second Manassas. The result was a full court-martial of Porter, which was to start in late November. The court was formed by some of Porter's most fervent opponents in the administration. Though General Henry Halleck was the one overseeing the affair, Secretary of War Edwin Stanton had significant influence over who sat on the commission. When the list of names was released, Brigadier General James Garfield was on it.

By the time Garfield was named to the Porter court-martial, he had been in Washington for over two months and was a congressman-elect. In early October, Garfield had won election to the House of Representatives, beating his opponent by nearly seven thousand votes out of the roughly twenty thousand that were cast. He won all five counties in his district in a decisive victory. Because the next Congress would not meet for another year still, Garfield had time to continue his military service, which he had stated was his intention to do. While he still expected an assignment in the field, being named to the Porter court-martial would keep him in Washington for the time being.[147]

Garfield did not enter the Porter trial as an unbiased and impartial observer. For months, he had filled his letters with harsh words regarding George McClellan, and Porter was McClellan's closest friend in the army. Furthermore, he already had a vested interest in defending one of the key players from the Second Manassas drama. Soon after the battle, with allegations of treason and incompetence being thrown at him, Irvin

McDowell had asked to be relieved of his command and for a court of inquiry to investigate his actions, hopefully clearing his name. In early October, McDowell asked Garfield to meet with him regarding the matter. Even before speaking with him, Garfield stated in a letter to Lucretia that the general had been "greatly wronged" by allegations of improper conduct. His conversation with McDowell only further solidified this belief. Indeed, Garfield wrote a lengthy defense of McDowell following their meeting, subscribing to McDowell's account of the campaign and displaying a strong bias against Fitz John Porter. The statement, written in early October, was riddled with inaccuracies, displaying Garfield's already developed opinions on the major players from Second Manassas weeks before he was named to the court-martial. He declared his loyalty to McDowell—"That he is a true brave man I have no doubt"—while stating that Pope had been treated

Secretary of War Edwin Stanton. *Library of Congress.*

treacherously by McClellan and his cabal, including Fitz John Porter. Adding in the fact that Garfield was living with Republican Salmon Chase at the time, it is clear that his name was added to the court-martial roster not to be an impartial judge but rather to impart his already developed opinions on the case. Indeed, the entire court was believed to have been created with one purpose in mind. "The court was chosen by Secretary Stanton and was organized to convict," wrote journalist A.K. McClure.[148]

The court-martial convened in early December, with hearings beginning officially on December 4. Garfield was certainly not the only Republican who would be hearing the case. The president of the court was David Hunter, a general who was so strongly in favor of abolition that earlier in 1862 he had issued a military order freeing slaves in the area commanded by his troops. Among the other officers were Major General Ethan Allen Hitchcock, Brigadier General Benjamin Prentiss, Brigadier General Silas Casey, Brigadier General Napoleon Buford, Brigadier General Rufus King, Brigadier General James Ricketts and Brigadier General John Slough. King and Ricketts were present at Second Manassas and thus were not impartial in the matter, and Casey had been rejected for a command in the Fifth Corps by Porter earlier that year. Joseph Holt was the judge advocate prosecuting the case, and Porter selected for his defense Reverdy Johnson, a former attorney general who represented Dred Scott in the infamous 1857 Supreme Court case.[149]

The charges against Porter were that, on numerous instances, he had disobeyed direct orders and had abandoned his post and withdrawn his men in the face of the enemy at Second Manassas. The witnesses who appeared during the trial provided damning testimony against Porter. Among them were Pope and McDowell, each of whom stood to benefit considerably by placing the blame of defeat elsewhere. The prosecution presented its case for several weeks, and it was not until late December that the defense began its arguments. There was little—if anything—that Reverdy Johnson could do at that point. Weeks earlier, during McDowell's testimony, Garfield had informed Rhodes that Pope's testimony was "direct and crushing" in its effect on Porter. A few days later, Garfield wrote to Hinsdale that the court-martial "is developing an exceedingly rich chapter of history, which will some day be read with great interest."[150]

On January 10, one year to the day after Garfield's battlefield victory at Middle Creek, the Porter court-martial proceedings came to a close. In a letter to his mother, Garfield described the trial as "laborious and searching," adding that there were over nine hundred pages of testimony and records. After the arguments came to a close on that day, the court deliberated for only three hours. There was little to discuss. For most of the judges, their decisions were already made. Porter was found guilty on both charges against him. He was to be cashiered out of the army and prohibited from ever again serving in a Federal office. The findings were passed on to President Lincoln, who had to approve them before the sentence could be made public. On January 21, 1863, Lincoln approved the verdict. Porter's military career was over.[151]

Several things are clear upon examining the case of Fitz John Porter. His actions at Second Manassas, despite the findings of the court, were not treacherous, and he did not deserve the fate that befell him. The man most responsible for Federal defeat at Second Manassas was John Pope, not Porter. Yet in the politically charged climate of Washington in the fall of 1862, facts on the battlefield came second to the divisiveness that had seized the Army of the Potomac. While he was not guilty on the battlefield, Fitz John Porter was guilty on a far different count: not only was he a close friend and ally of George McClellan's, but he also embraced the conservative political approach to the war that angered so many radical Republicans in Washington. It was this more than anything else that led to his conviction and dismissal from the army in January 1863.[152]

It is unfortunate that the Porter trial was part of Garfield's Civil War career. While the Porter verdict was later reversed, Garfield himself never wavered in his belief in Porter's guilt. Years later, in a letter to John Pope, Garfield confidently stated, "No public act with which I have been connected was ever more clear to me than the righteousness of the finding of that court." Other judges, including Benjamin Prentiss, also later expressed the belief that the court had done a fair and admirable job in delivering an honest verdict. The case and its implications lingered for years, and in 1878, President Rutherford B. Hayes reopened the matter. An 1879 board chaired by General John Schofield investigated the case and sent a recommendation to the president that he overturn the Porter verdict and reinstate him to the army because he was innocent of the charges. Even then, Garfield still refused to believe in Porter's innocence, writing to Jacob Cox, "I have been so stung by the decision that it is very hard to trust my own mind to speak of it." He spoke out on the House floor, declaring that if the verdict was overturned and Porter reinstated to the army, it would tarnish the reputations of the leading figures of the Lincoln administration and the Republican Party during the war. Garfield took his opinions on Porter with him to his grave in 1881, even as other veterans of the war—including Ulysses S. Grant—came out in support of Porter. After Garfield's death, his successor, President Chester Arthur, commuted Porter's sentence, and Congress allowed him to return to the army, restoring his rank. Though Porter received no back pay, his verdict was finally overturned. Despite this, Porter and his family carried disdain for Garfield for years afterward. According to one account, during the trial Garfield embraced the defendant, wrapping him in his arms and telling him not to worry, only to then vote in favor of his conviction, making Garfield an object of particular scorn for Fitz John Porter in the trial's aftermath.[153]

The Porter trial had a lingering effect on Garfield through the rest of his life. Not only was he deeply involved in the debate over Porter's innocence until his death, but Garfield also developed friendships and connections as a result of the trial. One of the strongest and longest-lasting friendships was with McDowell, who was exonerated by the court of inquiry he requested in 1862. McDowell and Garfield formed a strong bond, so much so that in 1870 James and Lucretia named their fifth child together Irvin McDowell Garfield.

No sooner had the Porter trial concluded than the next chapter of Garfield's military career began. In early January, Secretary of War Edwin Stanton indicated to Garfield that with the trial coming to an end, he would finally be bound for the battlefield once again. Having been in Washington for several months, it was time for Garfield to go back into active service in the field, which was his strong and fervent wish. Garfield was well liked by members of the Lincoln administration, and it was that, as well as his strong reputation in the field, that gained him a new opportunity in the field and a ticket out of Washington in January 1863.

Just days after voting to convict Porter, Brigadier General James Garfield—now a congressman-elect—departed for Tennessee and the Army of the Cumberland, where he was ordered to report to Major General William Rosecrans for his next assignment. After making a brief stop in Ohio to see Lucretia and Trot, Garfield made his way south. He rode into Rosecrans's camp in Murfreesboro, Tennessee, on January 25, 1863, ready to once again take part in the war.

CHAPTER 7

With the Army of the Cumberland

JANUARY 1863–JULY 1863

The chess board is now indeed muddled and no man sees through it.
—*James A. Garfield*

William Starke Rosecrans was one of the most influential generals of the American Civil War. Born in 1819 in Delaware County, Ohio, Rosecrans did not come from money. Instead, his father ran a farm and a tavern store, and as a teenager, William worked as a store clerk. Rosecrans's father had a distinguished background of service; he was a veteran of the War of 1812 who had served on the staff of General William Henry Harrison. Young William would follow his father's example, pursuing a career in the military. After a meeting with Congressman Alexander Harper, Rosecrans proved himself impressive enough to garner an appointment to the U.S. Military Academy at West Point. There, he came into his own. He did well academically and graduated fifth in the distinguished class of 1842, one that was filled with future Civil War generals; he graduated alongside such future luminaries as James Longstreet, Earl Van Dorn, Daniel Harvey Hill and Don Carlos Buell, a man whom Rosecrans would come to replace twenty years later. After West Point, Rosecrans married Anna Elizabeth Hegeman and served in the Corps of Engineers.[154]

Rosecrans missed out on serving in the war with Mexico, instead working as a professor at West Point. In 1854, after having served on numerous engineering assignments across the country, he left the army and tried his hand at a number of civilian pursuits. Perhaps the most well-known story

Major General William S. Rosecrans. *Library of Congress.*

regarding Rosecrans's pre–Civil War years occurred when he was the president of an oil and kerosene company in Cincinnati in 1859. One of the company's lamps caught on fire and burned him badly, leaving scars on his face for the rest of his life.

As a West Point graduate and native of Ohio, the start of the Civil War brought Rosecrans back into military life. He was appointed colonel of the 23rd Ohio, a regiment that had two future presidents within its ranks: Rutherford B. Hayes and William McKinley. No sooner had Rosecrans reentered the army than his career began to rise. He became a brigadier general in May 1861 and commanded troops in western Virginia, garnering respect and increased responsibility. In 1862, he was sent to the western theater and served under Henry Halleck during the campaign for Corinth. In September 1862, Rosecrans commanded troops in the Iuka-Corinth Campaign under the direction of Ulysses S. Grant. While his actions in the campaign were not flawless, he contributed enough to the Federal victory that Northern papers praised him. Soon, a new command beckoned.

In the late summer months of 1862, while James Garfield was in Washington and Rosecrans was fighting in Mississippi, the Confederate Army of Tennessee, commanded by General Braxton Bragg, pushed north into central Kentucky. Don Carlos Buell responded with the Army of the Ohio, catching up with the Confederates at Perryville in early October. After the battle there, Confederates fell back into Tennessee. Despite the withdrawal of Southern troops from Kentucky soil, frustrations were mounting with Buell in Washington, as Lincoln, Stanton and then General-in-Chief Henry Halleck wanted a more decisive and aggressive commander for the Army of the Ohio. When looking to replace Buell, the administration turned to Rosecrans. In late October, Buell was relieved of his command, and Rosecrans was put in charge of what was soon renamed the Army of the Cumberland.

Just a few weeks after taking his new command, Rosecrans led Union forces southward from Nashville toward Murfreesboro, where Bragg's Confederate Army of Tennessee awaited. On December 31, 1862, Bragg launched an assault on Rosecrans and his army just north of Murfreesboro along the banks of Stones River, and one of the bloodiest battles of the Civil War began. In the cold December air, Rosecrans was in the thick of the fight, riding along his lines and trying to repulse the Confederate attacks and save his army. January 1, 1863, saw a break in the action, and on January 2, Federals repulsed a final Confederate attack, ending the battle and forcing Bragg to fall back from Murfreesboro. With over twenty-four thousand casualties, Stones River ushered in the new year of 1863 with death and suffering on the fields of Tennessee.

While Stones River was a key victory for Federals in central Tennessee at a time when the Union desperately needed success somewhere, perhaps more important for James Garfield was one of the casualties who fell on December 31. As Rosecrans was riding his lines, a Confederate artillery shell decapitated his chief of staff, Julius Garesche, splattering the commanding general's uniform with blood and pieces of flesh. Born in Cuba and a member of the West Point class of 1841, Garesche had years of military experience and was a close personal friend of Rosecrans. His death left the army commander stunned and in need of a new officer to fill a crucial void on his staff. As it turned out, Garfield was arriving in his camp just when Rosecrans was looking for a new chief of staff. Over the course of the next year, Garfield would become forever linked to Rosecrans and the Army of the Cumberland. Indeed, no other Civil War general is so closely associated with Garfield's Civil War career—for better or worse—than William Rosecrans.

Rosecrans and Garfield did not seem to be well matched for working together or becoming close friends. The commanding general was filled with energy, evincing a kinetic nervousness that infused his actions. He was up until midnight or later, normally rising at eight o'clock. A salient feature of his persona was his strong faith. Rosecrans was a Roman Catholic in an army of Protestants. Despite his notorious reputation for using profanity when angered, his piety was a defining feature of Rosecrans as a general and as a man. His daily prayers were as regular and pressing as was the need for him to lead his army.

Upon first speaking with Rosecrans, Garfield was deeply impressed with his new commander. "General Rosecrans thinks rapidly and strikes forward into action with the utmost confidence in his own judgment," he informed Lucretia. In this decisiveness, Garfield saw a strong contrast between Rosecrans and the timid George McClellan. On a personal note, Garfield described Rosecrans as "the most Spanish looking man I know of…though he swears fiercely, yet he is a Jesuit of the highest style of Roman piety." Rosecrans apparently remembered Garfield from his actions in the Big Sandy Valley Campaign, and the first night Garfield was in camp, the two spoke until after midnight. This began a pattern for Garfield, who was not used to keeping such late hours. Rosecrans saw in the thirty-one-year-old general an intellectual partner, someone with whom he could discuss grand matters of religion, politics and military strategy. Garfield's background as a preacher, professor and politician certainly appealed to Rosecrans.[155]

The second night he was in camp, Rosecrans and Garfield ended up speaking past three o'clock in the morning. Writing to Harry Rhodes, Garfield related his conversation with the general and a few deeper impressions of the man. The two men "discussed a great range of questions of war, government, and religion," with Rosecrans displaying "muscular thoughts" on each topic. "I do not think him a great man in the sense of being [a] comprehensive and profound thinker," Garfield continued, "but for sharp, clear sense, ready, decisive judgment and bold reliant action he is certainly very admirable and hence an effective, successful general." The two men discussed the Bible, doctrines of the Roman Catholic Church and the difference between blasphemy and profanity, all of which Garfield said was "exceedingly interesting."[156]

Garfield had arrived in camp excited about his return to the front lines of the war, expecting to soon be given a brigade or division command in the Army of the Cumberland. In a goodbye letter to Chase, he expressed a belief that Tennessee, not Virginia, would be the scene of great battles and events. "I choose that field because I believe there is more life and work in the west and that the chief hope of the war rests on that army," Garfield wrote. However, while his relationship with Rosecrans grew, his enthusiasm for a field command was put on hold. Several weeks went by when the only direction he received from Rosecrans involved discussions on matters of faith. By mid-February, this would change. Rosecrans admitted that while he had a division that Garfield could command, he instead preferred him to take the position of the slain Julius Gareshe as his new chief of staff. This was a position of incredible responsibility and power in the army, essentially having the task of executing the orders and wishes of the commanding general. Rosecrans wanted someone in this position who could provide "unity and strength" for the army in future campaigns. "General Rosecrans could not pay me a higher compliment, nor in any way express more confidence in me," Garfield told Lucretia. He believed that by acting as Rosecrans's "alter ego" he could be of tremendous service to the army and the country, even more so than as a division commander. After thinking it over, Garfield accepted and immediately became one of the key figures of the Army of the Cumberland in 1863. During the War of 1812, Rosecrans's father had served on the staff of future president William Henry Harrison; now, during the Civil War, Rosecrans would have a future president on his own staff in 1863.[157]

Less than a month after he arrived in Murfreesboro, Garfield had a prominent position with one of the most important Union armies in the field. Soon after assuming his new title, Garfield wrote a long letter to Chase in Washington. Rosecrans was "sound to the bone on the question of the war and the way it should be conducted," Garfield believed. His faith in the general was in no small way influenced by Rosecrans's own "muscular religionness," as Garfield put it. "If the war and the government will stand by me I feel sure that he will justify their high expectations." From his letters to Chase and others, it appears as though he and Rosecrans were off to a great start working together.[158]

Throughout the next six months, Garfield and Chase corresponded frequently. Because of Garfield's status with Rosecrans and his close ties to Chase and other Republicans, he became an intermediary, conveying the behind-the-scenes operations and his personal opinions regarding the army to Washington. At first, this benefited all parties involved. However, with the slow pace of the war in Tennessee for most of 1863, Garfield became increasingly frustrated with his situation. His letters to Chase became an outlet, showing what Garfield was experiencing throughout his time with the Army of the Cumberland.

Before Garfield could settle into his new role, he first had to decide what to do about his election to Congress the previous fall. He had promised the voters of his district that if he were elected he would serve in the army until the time that the new congressional session met. Now that it was 1863, though Congress was not scheduled to meet until December, several members of Congress were writing to Garfield to encourage him to resign by March 4 so that he would not be in violation of any laws against holding a seat in Congress and being an active general in the army simultaneously. For clarification on the matter, Garfield wrote to several prominent Republicans and members of the Lincoln administration, including Attorney General Edward Bates. In late February, Bates responded by telling Garfield that there was no specific timetable for him to resign from the army, so long as he was no longer a general when he took his congressional seat, "taking care only that the duties of the two offices shall not clash." Thus, for the time being, Garfield could remain in the army, which was welcome news for both him and his new commander, William Rosecrans. Bates concluded his letter to Garfield by expressing his full confidence in Rosecrans after the general's victory at Stones River, saying that he and the president were looking to Rosecrans and his army "to restore the war in the southwest and renew the honor of the flag."[159]

While Garfield had a great passion for the war, he had also long acknowledged that he could not both remain in the army and serve as a congressman. The previous summer, when his friends and political allies were pressing for his nomination and election to Congress, Garfield had acknowledged the possibility of leaving the military for politics. In June 1862, he had written to a friend back home in Ohio that his military career was purely as a volunteer, not as a part of the standing regular army:

> *To remain in the army and follow the military as a profession was never any part of my plan. I have always intended and still intend to resign my*

commission as soon as the active work of the war is done. It seems to me that the successful ending of the war is the smaller of the two tasks imposed upon the government. There must be a readjustment of our public policy and management. There will spring up out of this war a score of new questions and new dangers. The settlement of these will be of even more vital importance than the ending of the war.

Thus, in 1863, when he joined the Army of the Cumberland, Garfield knew that his days in the military were numbered. While he had been elected to Congress, the work of the war was not yet done; up until he took his seat, he would make the most of the time he had and do everything in his power to finish the job.[160]

CHIEF OF STAFF

Garfield became the chief of staff for the Army of the Cumberland at a time when larger problems were developing in the Union war effort. Several weeks had passed since Rosecrans's victory at Stones River, and pressure was beginning to mount from the War Department for him to move south against Bragg's army. Certainly, Stones River had taken its toll on the Army of the Cumberland. Numerous commanders had been lost, creating command vacancies at all levels, including the one that Garfield assumed. Rosecrans believed that the army needed significant work in rebuilding and preparing for a new campaign. Henry Halleck and Edwin Stanton, along with President Lincoln, wanted continued pressure on Confederates in Tennessee. In the east, the Army of the Potomac was still in poor morale after the defeat at Fredericksburg in December 1862; to the west, Grant's Vicksburg Campaign was seemingly stalled. Amid these circumstances, there appeared to be an opportunity for Rosecrans to launch a new campaign against Bragg.

During this time, Rosecrans worked at building an army that was capable of the type of victory that Lincoln so desperately wanted. This was no easy task. While the army was at Murfreesboro, supplies were being shipped over two hundred miles by rail, and the Army of the Cumberland required sixty rail cars a day in order to feed both the soldiers and the animals the army relied on. Roughly seventy thousand soldiers needed 105 tons of food a day. Heavy rains in March further complicated this, as they hampered the cavalry patrols and excursions that Rosecrans was ordering to keep an eye on Bragg's position to the south. As March turned to April, winter gave way to spring in Tennessee, and the men remained where they had been since January. This time of inaction allowed the men to rest, and by the summer of 1863, the morale of the army was soaring.[161]

While Rosecrans did have good reason to rest his men after Stones River, the prolonged period of waiting that stretched on for months brought enormous pressure on him. Garfield was among those who, as of May, thought the army had been still long enough. Writing to Chase, Garfield expressed a belief in action, stating, "I am therefore for striking, striking, striking again 'till we do break them. The two armies here are in fine condition…there will be a fearfully bloody struggle when they grapple again." Garfield believed that soon enough a major campaign would be underway.[162]

Before the entire army moved, there were events going on in the field that did demand Garfield's attention. Confederate cavalry was a constant threat in Tennessee, continuously harassing Federal supply lines. Responding in kind, Garfield took part in organizing and planning a cavalry raid behind Confederate lines that was meant to damage Southern supplies and resources. Led by Colonel Abel Streight, the raid was launched in late April, and while it was well intentioned, it met a disastrous end. Streight and his men were slowed by heavy rain and hampered by Confederate cavalry. Having gone well over one hundred miles on the raid into Alabama, Streight was forced to surrender his command when pursued by Confederates and cut off from supplies.[163]

The failure of the Streight raid did little to assuage the difficult relationship that was developing between Rosecrans and Washington. The War Department had grown tired of receiving requests for more supplies and men, and the dispatches from each side grew increasingly terse. Garfield was caught in the middle of this tension. He repeatedly tried to soften Rosecrans's responses to Washington despite actually sharing some of the same concerns that Halleck and Stanton were conveying to Murfreesboro. In early May in Virginia, Union forces under Joseph Hooker suffered a dramatic defeat at Chancellorsville, once again leaving the hopes for Union success with Rosecrans in Tennessee and Grant outside Vicksburg. Worries persisted that if Rosecrans did not act, Bragg would send troops to reinforce Confederates fighting Grant in Mississippi. Rosecrans argued that by not acting, he was ensuring that his army would not be defeated. Should the Army of the Cumberland falter, Rosecrans reasoned, then the weight of Confederate forces in the West could be concentrated against Grant. In the midst of this pressure on Rosecrans, Lincoln wrote to him personally to insist something be done soon: "I would not push you to any rashness, but I am very anxious that you do your utmost, short of rashness, to keep Bragg from getting off to help Johnston against Grant."[164]

Throughout this time, Garfield was extremely busy at Rosecrans's headquarters. As chief of staff, his role was vital in maintaining a functioning army. He issued orders on Rosecrans's behalf, corresponded with generals regarding daily tasks and orders and helped to maintain organizational cohesion in the army command. Even the relative inaction of the army still required an enormous amount of work in issuing orders for patrols, dealing with issues of organization and military discipline and ensuring that

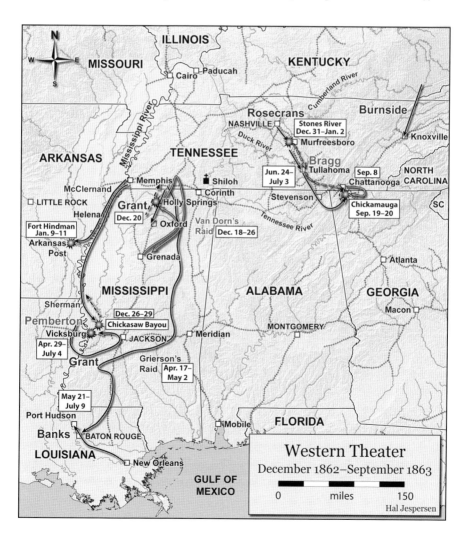

Rosecrans's wishes were carried out. On top of this, in May Garfield drew up and submitted to Rosecrans a plan for moving forward against Bragg. The Confederates were spread out across southern Tennessee, guarding the surrounding roads, mountain gaps and railroads north of Tullahoma. Garfield's plan was not to move directly against the Confederates but, rather, use deception and threaten the supplies of Bragg's Army of Tennessee. The plan formed the nucleus of what became the Tullahoma Campaign, though it would not begin for several more weeks.

Facing intense scrutiny, and fearful of the consequences a defeat might bring for himself, the army and the country, Rosecrans decided to poll his commanders about what he should do. A confidential memo was sent out to high-ranking officers in the army on June 8 asking several questions: first, did they believe that Bragg's force had already been weakened in order to assist Rebel armies elsewhere; second, did they believe that beginning a new campaign would prevent Bragg from potentially reinforcing Joseph Johnston in his fight against Grant; and third and most importantly, did they think it "advisable" for the army to advance. While the generals all responded in writing, Rosecrans also held a meeting on June 9 to gauge their opinions in person. During this council of war, Rosecrans also asked if the army could reasonably fight a battle and win and if advancing sooner rather than later might impact their odds. As the chief of staff, Garfield was present at the meeting, but because he did not have a command in the field, he did not have a say on the matter at hand. Instead, he took notes and recorded what occurred, remaining off to the side with newspaper reporter James Gilmore.[165]

If Rosecrans was expecting a confirmation of plans to advance, he was sorely mistaken once the meeting began. After months of waiting in Murfreesboro, gathering supplies and reorganizing the army, Rosecrans's subordinates in the Army of the Cumberland still did not think it wise to advance against Bragg's force. While a few of the generals believed that Bragg had indeed been weakened, everyone polled—a total of seventeen division and corps commanders—said that it was not wise to begin a new campaign at that time. Despite the flood of messages urging a movement that Halleck and Stanton had sent to Rosecrans in the previous months, clearly it was not just Rosecrans who thought it unwise to launch a new campaign in June. The consensus seemed to be that it was best to wait to see what became of Grant's Vicksburg operations before moving forward. Within a few days, Rosecrans passed this information on to Halleck, telling him that it was unwise to risk a campaign under the current conditions.[166]

During the weeks preceding this, Garfield had filled his letters home with suggestions that soon the army would be undertaking a new campaign. However, having witnessed firsthand such a definitive statement against advancing, Garfield grew frustrated and despondent in the days following the meeting. On June 11, he wrote to Harry Rhodes to describe "a sense of disappointment and mortification" that had overtaken him. "Now I write to tell you that I have given up all hopes of either dying or fighting at present." Having drawn up plans for a campaign and gotten initial approval from Rosecrans, the rejection by the officers of the army greatly affected Garfield. "The chess board is now indeed muddled and no man sees through it," he lamented.[167]

Because he did not have a chance to voice his opinions on the matter, Garfield wrote a lengthy letter to Rosecrans on June 12, laying out the reasons the army should move forward on a new campaign. He attempted to refute some of the points offered by officers against such a movement, noting that according to the intelligence received, Bragg's army was weaker in June than it had been before. Waiting for operations to develop around Vicksburg posed the risk of allowing Confederates to reinforce Bragg once the fighting subsided in Mississippi, further complicating the challenge of capturing Bragg's army. Garfield believed, as did the Lincoln administration, that Bragg's army was their true target. Moving against it, and soon, offered the best hope of victory in the field. "The Government and the War Department believe that this army ought to move upon the enemy," Garfield pleaded. "The army desires it, and the country is anxiously hoping for it." Garfield took care to note his agreement with Rosecrans's actions thus far, stating that it was wise to rest the army as long as he had. Yet the time for action had now arrived. Defeating Bragg's army would "crush the shell" of the Confederacy, leading, in turn, to the "collapse of the rebel Government." Garfield concluded his letter with a passionate call to action, writing, "For these reasons, I believe an immediate advance of all our available forces is advisable, and under the providence of God will be successful."[168]

Garfield's letter to Rosecrans was a remarkable statement by a chief of staff to his superior. It was the most important document he wrote during his military career. He was going out on a limb to express his opinions to a commander for whom he had always shown considerable respect. His letter was arguing not only with Rosecrans but also with the opinions of other esteemed generals in the army such as George Thomas, Phil Sheridan, Thomas Crittenden, Thomas Wood, David Stanley and others, all of whom had vastly more combat experience than he. Some have interpreted this letter as Garfield taking stock of the political winds and aligning himself with the wishes of the administration in Washington. Certainly, he did not lose any friends in the Lincoln administration with his views. Yet his private letters in the weeks leading up to this were filled with expressions of his desire for the army to move forward and crush the enemy. Garfield by nature had an aggressive view of the war. It is not surprising, therefore, that he disagreed with Rosecrans and favored a strong campaign by the Army of the Cumberland in June 1863.

Because he was going against the grain of the army, Garfield's opinions were not well received by some of the veteran generals. David Stanley believed that Garfield had no standing to write such a letter because he was not a troop commander and his views had not been solicited. Rosecrans later speculated that the document was drawn up to criticize his generalship. Others have seen Garfield's arguments quite differently. Famed war correspondent Whitelaw Reid described Garfield's letter as "the ablest military document known to have been submitted by a Chief of Staff to his superior during the war. General Garfield stood absolutely alone…[b]ut his statements were so clear and his arguments so forcible that he carried conviction."[169]

While some of the generals may have disapproved of Garfield's plea for action, soon enough they would be moving regardless of their own personal views. On June 16, Halleck demanded a decision from Rosecrans on an immediate movement. Realizing that perhaps the patience of Washington was at an end, Rosecrans resolved to advance within a few days' time. That same week, word arrived that it would only be a matter of time before Grant would seize Vicksburg, giving Rosecrans further encouragement to begin his campaign. Final preparations were put in place, and by the morning of June 24, telegraph wires finally carried news of an advance to Washington. That morning, Thomas Crittenden, commander of the 21st Corps, angrily confronted Garfield over his arguments in favor of action, accusing him of being responsible for the army's movement. "I wish you to understand that it is a rash and fatal move, for which you will be held responsible," Crittenden exclaimed. Hindsight would prove Crittenden quite wrong. The campaign upon which the army was embarking—and which he accused Garfield of being responsible for—was the Tullahoma Campaign, which is regarded by historians today as one of the finest and most successful campaigns of the Civil War's western theater.[170]

TULLAHOMA

Over the next nine days, Union soldiers spread out across the roads between Murfreesboro and Tullahoma, pressing Confederate forces at numerous key points. Rosecrans's nearly seventy thousand men advanced on Bragg's position along the Duck River, moving against four key gaps in the terrain to prevent Confederates from concentrating on any one advancing column. The plan of advance was very similar to what Garfield had done at Paintsville in the Big Sandy Valley in January 1862. The numerous Federal columns were meant to confuse Bragg and disguise the Federals' true intentions. While intimating an attack on the Confederate left flank with David Stanley's cavalry and Major General Gordon Granger's Reserve Corps, Rosecrans sent Major General Thomas Crittenden and his corps along roads leading toward McMinnville and the Confederate right flank. Moving toward the Confederate center were the corps of Major General George Thomas and Major General Alexander McCook, pushing toward Manchester just south of the Duck River. Within just a few days, Bragg was forced to pull his defensive lines back all the way to Tullahoma, where the army had been headquartered since its defeat at Stones River the previous January.[171]

With Confederate forces retreating, the campaign was off to considerable success. Garfield was enthusiastic, and he believed that greater opportunity

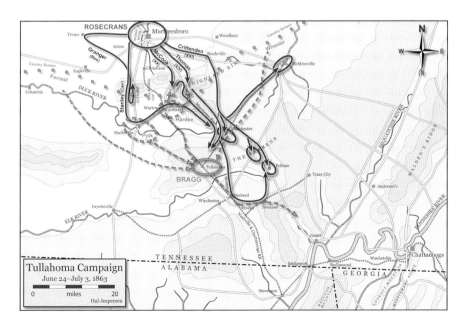

Tullahoma Campaign
June 24–July 3, 1863

0   miles   20
Hal Jespersen

was still possible. "We shall push for Tullahoma and try to get in their rear," Garfield wrote to Lucretia. "If we succeed we shall then test the metal [*sic*] of both armies." On June 29, as Federals continued their lines of march, Garfield believed that the campaign was "successful beyond the expectations of everyone outside headquarters" and that the Confederate retreats vindicated his lengthy letter to Rosecrans earlier that month.[172]

Yet everything was not perfect for the Federals. Heavy rains poured into southern Tennessee, making moving an army a nearly impossible task. Deluges of rain turned the roads into mud that was, as Rosecrans described it, "so soft and spongy that wagons cut into it as if it were a swamp." Seventeen days of continuous rains greatly impacted the ability of Federal troops to fully capitalize on the threat they posed to Bragg. One Federal division, commanded by Major General Thomas Wood, took five days to cover just twenty-one miles while marching on these muddy roads.[173]

Nonetheless, despite these difficulties, progress was being made. By the night of June 30, it had become clear to Braxton Bragg that, while he had intended to fight Rosecrans at Tullahoma, the movements of the Federal army were such that if the Confederates stayed where they were, they might be cut off from their route of supply and escape. That evening, Bragg began pulling his infantry out of Tullahoma, and by July 3, he had determined to fall back all the way to Chattanooga. By July 9, Bragg and his Army of Tennessee were in Chattanooga, south of the Tennessee River, having relinquished central Tennessee to William Rosecrans and his Army of the Cumberland.[174]

The Tullahoma Campaign was an incredible success. Through heavy rains, the Federals had gained a vast portion of Tennessee and forced Bragg into a perilous position while sustaining an extremely low loss in casualties. In the same summer that saw enormous bloodshed at Chancellorsville in Virginia and Gettysburg in Pennsylvania, the Army of the Cumberland proved that it was possible to seize important strategic ground without heavy losses. During this week-and-a-half campaign, Federal forces lost fewer than six hundred casualties, an astonishing statistic. Lincoln was impressed with the campaign, describing it as "the most splendid piece of strategy I know of." Rosecrans's cavalry commander, David Stanley, believed "[n]o better example of successful strategy was carried out during the war." Despite the rain preventing the complete destruction of the Confederates, Rosecrans had achieved great success.[175]

While many were pleased with Rosecrans, events transpiring elsewhere that same week placed the Tullahoma Campaign on the backburner for the attention of the nation. On July 3, Confederate general Robert E. Lee and his Army of Northern Virginia went down to a major defeat at Gettysburg, Pennsylvania. The following day, Ulysses S. Grant accepted the surrender of thousands of Confederates at Vicksburg, and the Confederacy effectively lost control of the Mississippi River. In light of these successes, each of which on its own would have eclipsed Tullahoma, the news of Rosecrans's victory in Tennessee was greeted with even greater expectations than ever before by Stanton. On July 7, the secretary of war wrote to Rosecrans, "You and your noble army now have the chance to give the finishing blow to the rebellion. Will you neglect the chance?" Stanton's note fit with the pattern of discord that had lingered between Rosecrans and the War Department for months. Even after Rosecrans had achieved credible results in the field, still he was patronized by Washington because no major battle had been fought. Irked by such a perceived lack of respect from Stanton, Rosecrans replied by defending the accomplishments of his command: "I beg in behalf of this army that the War Department may not overlook so great an event because it is not written in letters of blood."[176]

Soon enough, because of the urging of Washington, Rosecrans and his army would indeed take part in a major battle, and James Garfield was to be right in the middle of it. Thus far in the Civil War, Garfield had traveled hundreds of miles. He had raised a regiment, fought in the Big Sandy Valley, marched through the rain to Shiloh, endured the summer heat of the Deep South, taken part in political fights in Washington and helped the Army of the Cumberland achieve one of the great successes of 1863. His career had taken him to Kentucky; Tennessee; Mississippi; Alabama; Washington, D.C.; and Tennessee once again. Within a few weeks, he and the Army of the Cumberland would be moving south into the state of Georgia. While Garfield had been in the state briefly in the summer of 1862, this stay was to be much more consequential. He and the army were headed for battle along a small creek called Chickamauga, a fight that was destined to be "written in letters of blood" as the costliest and perhaps most savage battle in the western theater of the Civil War.

CHAPTER 8

To Chickamauga and Back

I am doing a work here for which I shall never get a tithe of the credit that others
will. Let it pass. I am glad to help save the republic.
—James A. Garfield

Despite the success of the Tullahoma Campaign, Garfield was not completely satisfied with the Army of the Cumberland's progress that summer. Certainly, its soldiers had shown themselves capable of doing great things. They had pushed Braxton Bragg back into Chattanooga and reclaimed central Tennessee for the Union, all at a low loss of life. Yet more and greater tasks would lie ahead for the battle-hardened and weary men of the Army of the Cumberland. Their adversary—the Army of Tennessee—had not yet been destroyed; Braxton Bragg still posed a threat for Rosecrans and his army. Another campaign was still necessary for Rosecrans to dispatch Bragg and seize the crucial city of Chattanooga.

During the Civil War, for both Union and Confederate forces, Chattanooga was as imposing a challenge to conquer as it was an indispensable location to hold. The city sat along the Tennessee River, nestled in the Cumberland Plateau of southern Tennessee, which historian Steven Woodworth described as "thirty miles of rugged, barren country with poor roads and virtually no food or fodder." Railroads connected the city to important locales such as Nashville, Knoxville and Atlanta, making it a vital rail hub for the southeastern Confederacy. Furthermore, being located along the Tennessee River meant that Chattanooga could flourish as a center of industry;

crucial raw materials and products were manufactured there and sent along the numerous transportation lines to other parts of the Confederacy. For Southern forces, holding the city meant securing transportation highways and blocking any Federal advance into northern Georgia. For the Union army, occupying Chattanooga would damage Southern infrastructure and provide a crucial supply base from which further campaigns southward could be launched. For these reasons and more, few cities in the Confederacy were more important to the fate of each side than Chattanooga.[177]

With more work still to be done, the immediate aftermath of the Tullahoma Campaign saw continued discord between Rosecrans and Washington. Halleck and Stanton recognized that Bragg's army was still a danger, and they demanded that action be taken to eliminate it. On July 24, three weeks after Rosecrans's army had entered into Tullahoma, General-in-Chief Halleck sent the general a strongly worded message about what was expected of him. "The patience of the authorities here has been completely exhausted," Halleck wrote. "If I had not repeatedly promised to urge you forward, and begged for delay, you would have been removed from the command." Halleck compared Rosecrans's circumstances to those facing his predecessor Don Carlos Buell, who had been relieved the previous October for failing to aggressively pursue Bragg after fighting in Kentucky. He urged him "as a friend" to advance soon because "the pressure for your removal has been almost as strong as it has been in his [Buell's] case." The following day, Halleck again prodded Rosecrans, telling him to push Bragg from Tennessee before he could be reinforced: "The pressure for this movement at this time is so strong that neither you nor I can resist it." With such strong urgings from Washington, Rosecrans certainly realized he would be forced to move sooner rather than later.[178]

In the midst of these circumstances, General James Garfield's long-simmering frustrations over the army's slow pace boiled over in a letter to Chase on July 27, in which he reflected on the six months that had passed since he joined the Army of the Cumberland. Since the previous January, "enormous and highly important labor" had been undertaken in preparing the army for a new active campaign. Indeed, by Garfield's own judgment it was not until the previous May that the army could have conceivably been ready for action in the field. As a result of these improvements, Garfield believed that the Army of the Cumberland was "by far the best the country has ever known," yet the delays of the spring and summer left him deeply concerned about the attitude among the army's leading generals. Once the army finally moved on Tullahoma, it did so only after Garfield had urged

Rosecrans to act. While heavy rains and muddy roads had prevented them from crushing Bragg's force, if the army had moved sooner, as Garfield had suggested, then the weather would not have been a problem, and "the army of Bragg would in all human probability no longer exist." Even after the recent success—limited as he believed it was—Garfield wanted more action from Rosecrans.

> *I have since then urged with all the earnestness I possess a rapid advance… Thus far the General has been singularly disinclined to grasp the situation with a strong hand and make the advantage his own. I write this with more sorrow than I can tell you for I love every bone in his body and next to my desire to see the rebellion blasted is my anxiety to see him blessed, but even the breadth of my love is not sufficient to cover this almost fatal delay. My personal relations with Gen. Rosecrans are all that I could desire. Officially I share his counsels and responsibilities even more than I desire, but I beg you to know that this delay is both against my judgment and my every wish.*

Garfield made clear that while he preferred to be in the field, he loathed the lack of aggressive action so much that he would consider leaving Rosecrans's staff: "Pleasant as are my relations here, I would rather command a Battalion that would follow and follow and strike and strike than to hang back while such golden moments are passing…If this inaction continues long, I shall ask to be relieved and sent somewhere where I can be part of a working army."[179]

Certainly, Garfield's letter to Chase in late July was of questionable judgment. He was speaking ill of his commanding officer behind his back to authorities in Washington who already had reason to dislike Rosecrans. Whether justified or not, the many months it took Rosecrans to follow up his victory at Stones River with a new campaign did not earn him any friends or admirers in the Federal capital. Garfield's private messages to Chase certainly did not help him any on that count. Yet Garfield's letter does not assume the tone or tenor of a missive sent for personal and political gain, nor does it contain any contempt or maliciousness. Indeed, taken collectively, the letters that Garfield sent to Chase during 1863 more closely resemble letters from a general and congressman-elect in the army to a friend and mentor whom he greatly admired. After all, Chase had taken Garfield in as his own when the young Ohioan spent the later months of 1862 in the capital. Garfield's letters still expressed his admiration for Rosecrans while also voicing his frustrations over a lack of more aggressive action. From the beginning of the war, Garfield maintained a consistent belief that nothing but strong, decisive and aggressive action against the South and the institution of slavery could save the Union. He continued that belief throughout his military career. And it was that belief, more than any political machination, that was the driving force behind his criticisms of Rosecrans and his malaise over the relative inaction of the Army of the Cumberland in 1863.

Rosecrans was certainly aware of Garfield's opinions regarding the need for aggressive action. Indeed, Garfield's own lengthy message to Rosecrans before the Tullahoma Campaign suggests he was not shy in sharing his thoughts with the commanding general. The two were known to enjoy a close working relationship, in which Rosecrans relied on Garfield's mind for assistance in both personal and professional matters. Rosecrans already knew that Washington was displeased with him, and he knew that Garfield was in tune with radical Republicans on matters of war policy. Thus, Garfield's letter to Chase in late July was not a treacherous backstabbing move but, rather, the venting of a frustrated officer to a friend and confidant in the capital. He made the same statements to Lucretia back home, telling his wife, "I don't feel at all satisfied with the slow progress we are making and I expect to hear complaints and just ones, soon. There are the strongest possible reasons for using every moment now before the rebels can recover from their late disasters."[180]

Soon enough, however, Garfield and the army would find themselves advancing again. In early August, after weeks of bickering, Halleck sent explicit orders telling Rosecrans to "move forward without delay." Rosecrans, with the backing of his senior corps commanders Thomas Crittenden and George Thomas, said he needed to wait until mid-August or else he would resign. Halleck agreed, and on August 16, a new campaign began.[181]

The immediate target of the new campaign was to seize Chattanooga. To accomplish this, Rosecrans was going back to what had worked before; he would once again rely on multiple routes of advance to disguise his intentions and force Bragg into making very difficult choices. Major General Thomas Crittenden, commanding the 21st Corps, was ordered to move toward Chattanooga itself through the northern passes of Sand Mountain; Major General George Thomas, who led the 14th Corps, was sent twenty-four miles south of Crittenden, where his men were to pass through Stevens's Gap. Even farther south was Major General Alexander McCook's 20th Corps, which marched to Winston's Gap, eighteen miles south of Thomas. Thus, Rosecrans had a distance of forty-two miles between the various infantry corps of his army, while his cavalry spread out in an attempt to screen the Federal efforts to cross over the Tennessee River. Rosecrans not only wanted

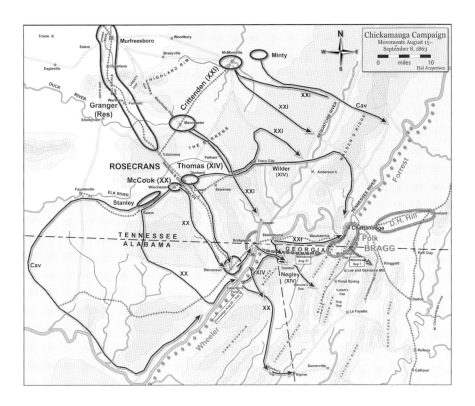

to move around Bragg's flank, but once south of the Confederates, he also intended to seize control of the Western and Atlantic Railroad, cutting Bragg off from resupply and reinforcement and enabling the capture of both the Confederate army and Chattanooga.[182]

As the chief of staff for the Army of the Cumberland, Garfield was to play a pivotal role in assisting Rosecrans with planning, issuing orders and overseeing the campaign. The timing was not good for him personally, however, as August saw the thirty-one-year-old Ohioan seized with another severe bout of diarrhea and sickness. His letters home to Lucretia told the tale of his struggle to remain with the army. "I am very weak but I am now, I hope, over the worst," he wrote on August 14. "I must go back to bed. I am urging a movement, and think I will be ready to accompany it." A week later, as the army began its new campaign, he told his wife how close he had come to missing out on the action. His cot was brought to the front near the Tennessee River, and as he slowly regained his strength, he looked ahead to the promises of new marches and movements. In doing so, he thanked Lucretia for her support and expressed a measure of selflessness, believing that his actions were not for personal acclaim but for the cause of the Union:

> *You came near having me at home…and nothing but my will and the great work before this army, in which the General says he don't know how to spare me, kept you and the little cogger from seeing me…There is so much of myself in the plan of this campaign that I must help realize my ideas. It looks now as though we should have a bloody crossing, but we may not. It is the greatest undertaking of the kind during this war. The river is from 500 to 900 yards wide and pretty deep, averaging ten feet. I appreciate what you say in regard to my work in this army and I thank you for the kind and loving words you wrote. I believe my army life has been as free from self-seeking and pride as any part of my whole life. I am doing a work here for which I shall never get a tithe of the credit that others will. Let it pass. I am glad to help save the republic.*[183]

Garfield believed that the new campaign offered tremendous possibilities, and the passage of another week saw him send another lengthy letter home laying out the importance of the army's current undertaking:

> *But I know you will appreciate the situation of affairs here when I tell you that all the fruits of the past operations of this army since I opened its first gun and won its first victory at Middle Creek are now about to be crowned or lost in a great and trying campaign beyond the mountains on the soil of Georgia. It is not vanity for me to say that no man in this army can fill my place during this movement. It would take him several months to learn the character and condition of affairs as I know them and to hold that influence with the commanding General that I do. For these reasons I believe I can more ably serve the country during this campaign than ever before in my life and anything short of breaking down my constitution and destroying my efficiency altogether I feel like doing to help carry out our plans.*[184]

As Federal forces spread out across Tennessee, Alabama and Georgia, Braxton Bragg and his Army of Tennessee were faced with a dilemma. While Bragg knew that the Federal army would have to split apart to pass through the mountains around Chattanooga, those same mountains would make it difficult for him to defend the city. An experienced military man, Bragg realized that he either had to leave Chattanooga or risk being pinned down by the sudden arrival of Rosecrans and his army. Having received reports of Union troops crossing the Tennessee River at numerous places, spreading out forty miles on either side of Chattanooga, Bragg opted to leave the city and head south. On September 8, the Union army saw trails of dust headed south from the city, signaling the Confederate retreat. Confederate deserters who painted a picture of a demoralized Confederate army also began coming into Union lines. As a result, Rosecrans issued new orders to his army. Crittenden's men were to head for Chattanooga. Thomas was to push through the mountains into McLemore's Cove, arriving in LaFayette, Georgia, where his corps could potentially threaten Bragg's retreat toward Rome. McCook's corps was ordered to swing far to the south in order to potentially cut off Bragg's retreat in the direction of Atlanta.[185]

Rosecrans sensed blood in the water. It appeared as though his follow-up to the Tullahoma Campaign was proceeding just as well as the original had. This time, however, there were no heavy rains to slow the Federal advance and allow the Confederates to slip away. Rosecrans was certain that the destruction of Bragg was within his grasp. He had only to close his hand and capture the prize. The caution that had gripped the Army of the Cumberland for so long was now thrown to the wind as the various corps were pushed through the mountains of northern Georgia in order to cut off Bragg's retreat and end the Army of Tennessee once and for all. Rosecrans was optimistic when he reported his progress to Washington: "Chattanooga is ours without a struggle, and East Tennessee is free. Our move on the enemy's flank and rear progresses, while the tail of his retreating column will not escape unmolested." In order to gain such a reward, Rosecrans had to gamble at considerable risk. If the Confederates were to stop along the way, they could possibly concentrate and strike any one part of the Union army before it could reunite as a whole. Rosecrans had forced Bragg from Chattanooga, but the tables would soon begin to turn against him.[186]

Unbeknownst to the Union high command, the lengthy delays of July and August had allowed the Confederacy time to pool its resources to assist Bragg's army. Parts of several different Confederate armies—including Robert E. Lee's Army of Northern Virginia—were ordered to Chattanooga to assist the Army of Tennessee. Knowing help would soon be arriving meant that Bragg could afford to consider offensive possibilities instead of simply retreating to Atlanta. The men of Major General Simon Buckner's command in eastern Tennessee had already joined forces with his, as had the division of Major General John Breckenridge. In addition to these troops, Bragg also knew that two divisions from the corps of Lieutenant General James Longstreet were on their way.[187]

Soon after falling back from Chattanooga, Bragg decided to turn on Rosecrans's advancing columns. The divided Federal army was an inviting target, and Bragg hoped to defeat it piecemeal as it came through the mountain passes. As George Thomas's men advanced toward LaFayette, Bragg ordered three divisions to strike them in McLemore's Cove. September 11 was a day of high tension on both sides. Delays and disagreements in the Confederate army prevented the crushing attack for which Bragg had hoped. Contact was made, however; Confederates did eventually move forward to hit the 14th Corps division of Major General James Negley. By that night, it was abundantly clear to the Federals that the situation was much different from what had been expected. Bragg was not leading a demoralized army on a retreat; instead, the Confederates were waiting for the Federals on the eastern side of the mountains.[188]

The Army of the Cumberland was caught off guard by these developments, as was Garfield. On September 10, Garfield had dismissed

Major General George H. Thomas. *Library of Congress.*

rumors of the Confederates concentrating for an attack, claiming they were "hardly worthy of a moment's consideration." Just two days later, George Thomas wrote to Garfield to tell of his encounter with Rebel infantry in McLemore's Cove, asking for reinforcements and stating that he was opposed by "a large part of Bragg's army." That same day, Thomas wrote to his staff, "Nothing but stupendous blunders on the part of Bragg can save our army from total defeat."[189]

Facing uncertain odds, Rosecrans quickly scrambled to send out orders concentrating the Army of the Cumberland near Chickamauga Creek. Because of the great distance between the various Union corps, this was not an easy task. It would take several days before the army was unified once again. In the meantime, word arrived from Halleck in Washington that Bragg was being reinforced by the men of Longstreet's command. Union reinforcements would be on their way as well, Halleck reported, but it was clear that help would not arrive soon enough. Having listened to the repetitive urgings of Washington to move forward instead of waiting for reinforcements and supplies, Rosecrans now found himself in exactly the type of predicament that he had feared. He would have to fight Bragg's army on his own, despite that army numbering nearly eighty thousand men by some accounts. In reality, the numbers were closer than what many on the Union side feared. When the Army of the Cumberland was finally united, it was roughly sixty-two thousand men strong. For the Southerners, once the reinforcements had arrived, the Army of Tennessee numbered over sixty-eight thousand. The coming Battle of Chickamauga would be a rarity in Civil War history; it was one of the only fights where the Confederates outnumbered the Federals.[190]

In the midst of this frenetic campaign, James Garfield recognized that a battle would soon take place. Having been dismissive of the Confederates a few days earlier, Garfield was under no such illusions anymore, writing to Rhodes on September 13 from Chattanooga: "I am just leaving for the center of the army 30 miles from here in Georgia. A battle is imminent. I believe the enemy now intends to fight us. He has a large force and the advantage in position. Unless we can outmaneuver him we shall be in a perilous position. But we will try."

A few days later, Garfield had time to write a letter to Lucretia before the fighting began. Noting that the odds of a Confederate success were greater now than ever before, Garfield's letter clearly laid out the situation facing the Army of the Cumberland:

Our army has the line of West Chickamauga Creek to the Northwest of LaFayette; half of our line [stands] with its back against Lookout Mountain. The situation is one of great interest and great results are depending on the outcome of the contest or retreat which must occur soon.

My health is improving as we advance…I think I shall get through the campaign without a broken constitution, though I think the war will have shortened my life a few years if not more than a few. Just at this point of my writing, a telegram has been received from Washington confirming the rumors we have already had that Longstreet has reinforced Bragg with three divisions from Lee's army, and that Sherman and Hurlbut have been ordered to the Tennessee River. This being so the day of the struggle will probably be deferred but it will be great when it comes. Thank God that the forces concentrating on both sides are being concentrated for a final struggle. It will, I believe, be the finishing great blow.[191]

Here, on the eve of the greatest battle of his military career, Garfield still displayed the enthusiasm for the war that he had projected as an Ohio state senator in April 1861. Two and a half years before, the then twenty-nine-year-old Garfield wrote that he would rather lose one million men in battle than see the Union surrender and fall to the rebellious South. Now, in September 1863, many miles, battles and casualties later, Garfield still believed that the suffering of battle was necessary to root out the evil of slavery and secession. The Battle of Chickamauga was about to begin, and James Garfield was to play an integral part.

CHICKAMAUGA: "THE HARDEST FOUGHT AND BLOODIEST BATTLE OF THE REBELLION"

September 18, 1863, saw the Army of the Cumberland concentrating and forming battle lines along the La Fayette Road, just west of Chickamauga Creek, in northwest Georgia. Rosecrans was attempting to maintain his defensive foothold in the area by slowly shifting his divisions and army corps to the left, extending his battle line northward so as to maintain and secure his connections with Chattanooga. While shifting northward, it would be essential to guard the La Fayette Road and the Dry Valley Road. If those routes were blocked, the army would be cut off and in danger of being destroyed. For the Confederates, that was precisely what Braxton Bragg had in mind.[192]

The Battle of Chickamauga, depicted in this sketch by Alfred Waud, had more casualties than any other battle in the western theater of the Civil War. *Library of Congress.*

Accordingly, Confederates attempted to cross the Chickamauga Creek at and around Reed's Bridge, northeast of Lee and Gordon's Mill, on the afternoon of September 18. The Confederates spread out to several crossing points, and fighting soon broke out between the two armies. These were the first shots of the Battle of Chickamauga. While Bragg had hoped to gain the left flank of the Federals, Rosecrans was moving to protect his own flank and threaten that of Bragg. That night, George Thomas's corps marched north to the Kelly Farm, located along the La Fayette Road, near a hill where George Washington Snodgrass and his family had built a cabin and a farmstead after moving to Georgia in the 1840s. By the morning of September 19, there were Federal troops in the path that Bragg had intended to attack. Confederate cavalry under Nathan Bedford Forrest clashed with men of Thomas's 14th Corps, and the fighting of the day before resumed.[193]

When the fighting began on the morning of September 19, Garfield was with Rosecrans at Union army headquarters, located at the Gordon-Lee Mansion, where the commanding general had been for the past few days. The sounds of Thomas's fight were rolling over the Georgia farm fields and woodlots, suggesting that the battle was growing in size and strength. With news that Bragg's army was concentrating for a full assault, and with

Thomas asking for assistance, Federal reinforcements were ushered into the fray shortly after 10:00 a.m.

As a result, Rosecrans soon left the Gordon-Lee Mansion and looked to move closer to the fight. With Garfield and the rest of his staff in tow, Rosecrans rode to the Widow Glenn house, where he and his staff set up a new headquarters location. Eliza Glenn was in her mid-twenties with two young children at the time. She had lost her husband to disease while he was serving in the Confederate army in the spring of 1863. According to war correspondent William Shanks, the family was worried by the presence of the Union army and the prospects of a major battle nearby. Garfield, "with the kindness of his great nature," briefly paused in his work of writing out dispatches and orders to speak to the family and comfort them. Rosecrans himself also spoke to the young widow, encouraging her to leave with her family before any harm came to them from the escalating battle nearby. While Eliza and her children soon left the house with a family slave, Rosecrans and his staff would remain. The Glenn house, a rather small log cabin, was situated on a hillside that offered a wide view of several parts of the Union battle line. Because of its elevation and central location behind Union lines, it was a fitting place for Rosecrans to remain during the fight. It was here where Garfield spent most of his time during the battle. By mid-morning, the dispatches that Garfield was sending out to army officers were labeled as coming from "Widow Glenn's."[194]

Though long relegated to the back pages of history in favor of the action on the following day, the fighting at Chickamauga on September 19 was noteworthy for the men of the Army of Tennessee and the Army of the Cumberland. The terrain of the northern Georgia battlefield made it so that the fight was preeminently one between individual regiments and brigades. The battle was hectic and confusing, leaving a lasting impression on all those who fought there.[195]

The fighting that day saw both Rosecrans and Bragg throwing increasing numbers of brigades and divisions into the contest. By mid-morning, Rosecrans began trying to strengthen his center and right as well, hoping to find a weak spot in the Confederate lines. With all of the moving divisions in the Army of the Cumberland, the order of command quickly became muddled. Garfield was in the midst of the confusion, rapidly writing orders to commanders on various parts of the field and using his insight and experience in working with Rosecrans to make sense of the commander's wishes. The orders that he sent on Rosecrans's behalf involved the slow and methodical shifting of the army northward while fending off various

Confederate assaults. With a flurry of dispatches emerging from his pen, Garfield was in the thick of the action for the Army of the Cumberland at Chickamauga. By mid-afternoon, Rosecrans was ordering up divisions from the Federal right to plug holes in the Union lines. By day's end, thousands had fallen as casualties, but the Army of the Cumberland was still intact, having survived a vicious day of battle.[196]

That evening, as darkness and cold temperatures gripped the battlefield landscape, Rosecrans held a council of war meeting at the Widow Glenn house. After discussing the events of the day, it was agreed that the Confederates had the numerical advantage in the fight. Nonetheless, the army was to stay and correct its position for the following morning. During this meeting, George Thomas discussed the fight of his corps, noting that he would likely need additional help in holding his position the next day, something that was crucial to Federal success at the battle. While Rosecrans was unsure of where exactly he would find reinforcements to do so, he was sure that strengthening the left was the right decision. He ordered the rest of the army to continue its process of slowly moving north toward Thomas while fending off the numerous Confederate assaults that were sure to resume in the morning. When the meeting came to a close, the generals dispersed into the cold night air. The headquarters staff, Garfield included, tried to get what sleep they could on the frigid floor of the cabin. For Garfield, the night of September 19, 1863, was spent the same way he had spent many of his young nights in northeast Ohio: trying to hide from the cold wind as it dove through the cracks in the log cabin around him.[197]

Across the enemy lines, Confederate forces were devising their own plans for the following day. Lieutenant General James Longstreet's command was arriving in significant numbers, strengthening Bragg's force for the next day's fight. In a rather unusual move, Bragg ordered the reorganization of the Army of Tennessee that night, splitting the forces between James Longstreet and Lieutenant General Leonidas Polk. Hoping to cut Rosecrans off from Chattanooga, the Confederate plan of attack for the following morning was for Polk to launch a massive attack into the Union left, with successive waves of Confederate attackers rolling southward and pounding the Union lines, hopefully pushing the Army of the Cumberland to its death by cutting it off from Tennessee. While Polk's assault would move forward in a piecemeal fashion the following morning, it was clear that the night of September 19 saw each army focusing its attention for the following day on the left flank of the Union army.[198]

September 20 dawned as the sun broke through the chilled morning air. Rosecrans began the day exhausted, a good night's rest having escaped him once again. No doubt the same exhaustion was shared by his staff, as the general's demeanor often affected those around him, including Garfield. Having begun the day with a Catholic Mass, Rosecrans took a few moments to observe the fields around his headquarters, enjoying a morning cigar before setting out on the business of the day. His demeanor left an impression on a writer from the *Cincinnati Commercial*, who noted:

> *I knew, for I had seen Rosecrans often under widely differing circumstances, that he was filled with apprehensions for the issue of that day's fight. I recognized a change instantly, although I could hardly say in what it consisted. Rosecrans is usually brisk, nervous, powerful of presence, and to see him silent or absorbed in what looked like gloomy contemplation, filled me with indefinable dread.*

As the early dawn spread across the battlefield, the sun peered through the mist. "The sky was red and sultry," Rosecrans recalled, "and the atmosphere and all the woods enveloped in fog and smoke." After morning Mass, Rosecrans, Garfield and the rest of the Union staff rode into the mist at 6:00 a.m., surveying and adjusting the battered lines of the Army of the Cumberland. During this ride, Garfield had the opportunity to survey the scenes of the previous day's fighting, witnessing firsthand the carnage of battle.[199]

At 9:30 a.m., the Confederates resumed their attacks from the day before, testing the Federal left flank along the La Fayette Road. With the weight of the Confederate attacks striking his lines, it was not long before Thomas needed additional support. Accordingly, he sent word to Brigadier General John Brannan for him to bring his division to his aid. Brannan was one of Thomas's division commanders, but Rosecrans had repositioned his men earlier that day without informing Thomas, creating a confusing situation on the field. Upon receiving his orders from Thomas, Brannan was unsure of what to do; he was concerned about leaving the right flank of Major General Joseph Reynolds's division unprotected. His departure would leave a gap in the Federal lines. While Brannan agreed to come to Thomas's assistance, word was sent to Rosecrans that Brannan's place needed to be filled. It was just before 10:45 a.m. when the matter came to Rosecrans's attention at Union headquarters. Needing to send out orders to fill what he believed was a gap in the Union line, Rosecrans

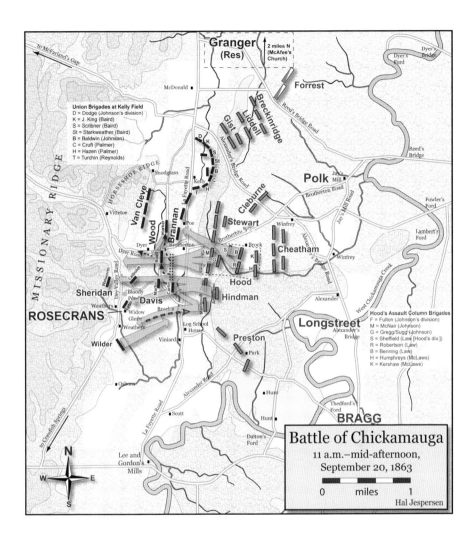

Battle of Chickamauga
11 a.m.–mid-afternoon,
September 20, 1863

0   miles   1

Hal Jespersen

turned not to Garfield, who was busy writing other orders, but to Major Frank Bond, an aide-de-camp. Rosecrans dictated a message to Bond, who quickly jotted it down, telling Brigadier General Thomas Wood to "close up on Reynolds as fast as possible, and support him." The message did not provide any additional instructions or clarifications, as Garfield's written dispatches so often did. There was no care exerted to remove any confusion, just the sparse wording of the order itself. Shortly after it was written, the message was given to Lieutenant Colonel Lyne Starling to carry to Wood, whose division was in the center of the Union line. This course of events was soon to prove disastrous.[200]

Despite not writing the order, Garfield was aware of it; he told Starling that he believed the measure was meant to replace Brannan in the line. Yet the way the order was written did not make clear that Wood was to move if—and only if—Brannan had already shifted his command. While Rosecrans had told Starling to verbally communicate that condition to Wood, the written order itself was lacking that clarity. Moreover, the order also suggested that Wood was to "close up on Reynolds," which meant move next to him in line, as well as "to support him," which meant form his line behind Reynolds. These were two contradictory objectives, which made the order very confusing.

By the time the soon-to-be fateful message left Union headquarters, the situation at the front was not at all what Rosecrans expected it to be. Thomas had canceled his orders to Brannan, and now Confederates were appearing to Brannan's front. Upon receiving the order from Rosecrans, Wood found the wording and intent to be very confusing. Because Brannan's division was still in line to Wood's left, in order to follow the order, Wood would have to withdraw his division and move it behind Reynolds to provide support. When Wood told Starling that Brannan's division was still in line, Starling responded that the order was meant to fill in a supposed gap in the line, one that apparently did not exist.

In the midst of these confusing events, Wood was uncertain of what to do. Earlier in the campaign, Wood had been harshly criticized by Rosecrans during the advance on Chattanooga. Not wanting another rebuke from the army commander, Wood asked Major General Alexander McCook, who was with him when he received the order, what he should do with the instructions. McCook, who himself was under scrutiny from Rosecrans at the battle, responded that the commanding officer likely knew something they did not, and it would be best to follow the instructions as written and to do so right away. According to Wood, McCook promised to bring forward a division to fill Wood's place in the line. Thus, with this in mind, Wood decided to follow his instructions specifically as written. Despite the growing crescendo of skirmish fire on his front, Wood pulled his division out of its place on the line shortly before 11:00 a.m.[201]

This incident became perhaps the greatest controversy of Chickamauga. Arguments over whether Rosecrans or Wood was to blame lasted for decades. Clearly, Rosecrans's order of battle had been so confused and muddled that a glaring error occurred as a result of an order that was not run through his chief of staff. Garfield was innocent in the matter, as he was sure to note in a report on his military service written in 1873, stating that he wrote every order for Rosecrans during the battle except for one. While Rosecrans told Starling to convey the verbal order to Wood as well, the written message was what Wood followed at the recommendation of McCook. Rosecrans's order to Wood, and Wood's compliance with it, created a gap precisely in the middle of the Union battle line.

The timing of these events could not have been worse for the Federals and better for the Confederates. Before Wood's division could fully pull out of its position in line, the command of James Longstreet thrust a dagger directly into the now weakened Union center, exploiting an opening that Federal soldiers had occupied just minutes before. Fifteen thousand Confederates poured into Federal lines, enveloping both the now weakened Union center as well as the Union

Brigadier General Thomas Wood. *Library of Congress*.

right flank. As the Confederate tide crashed into the Union line, there was nothing but Georgia farmland and a few Union infantry divisions to stop them from reaching Rosecrans's headquarters.[202]

Among those who were present at Union headquarters during the battle was Charles Dana, assistant secretary of war. Dana had been sent by the War Department to accompany Rosecrans and his staff during the campaign, likely so that Stanton could keep a close eye on the commander. Rosecrans had not taken well to Dana's presence—he bristled at any interference from the War Department—but he tolerated him in the field. Even so, many on Rosecrans's staff suspected Dana was "the spy of the War Department" whose purpose was to find cause to remove Rosecrans. Dana was present alongside Garfield for much of Chickamauga. He had been one of the officers who, like Garfield, spent the chilly night of September 19 in the Widow Glenn cabin. On the morning of September 20, as the Union headquarters was humming with activity, Dana found himself overcome by his lack of sleep from the previous nights and sat down in the grass to take a brief nap. As he recalled years later, his brief respite was soon interrupted: "I was awakened by the most infernal noise I ever heard. Never in any battle I had witnessed was there such a discharge of cannon and musketry. I sat up on the grass, and the first thing I saw was General Rosecrans crossing himself—he was a very devout Catholic. 'Hello!' I said to myself, 'if the general is crossing himself, we are in a desperate situation.'"[203]

Dana awoke to find soldiers from the Confederate Army of Tennessee pouring through the center of the Union line, headed straight for the Widow Glenn's farm and the Union headquarters. The same sights and sounds that roused Dana from his nap were seen by the entire Union high command. It was a moment that was nearly unparalleled in the war—the entire

Assistant Secretary of War Charles Dana, who was present with Rosecrans's headquarters staff during the Chickamauga Campaign. *Library of Congress.*

headquarters staff of an army was square in the path of a Confederate attack. Soon the hillside was peppered by exploding shells and bullets. In a moment of crisis, Rosecrans and his staff dissolved into the retreat of the Union army. "I was on my horse in a moment," wrote Dana, adding, "The headquarters around me disappeared."[204]

As the headquarters evaporated, Rosecrans and Garfield made their way toward Thomas, trying to push through the mob of demoralized soldiers. For the next hour, Rosecrans remained on the field, doing what he could to salvage the situation, with Garfield staying by his side. By noon, however, with the army falling apart around him, Rosecrans and his staff started for the Dry Valley Road, which was their escape toward Rossville and Chattanooga. As they rode west and north, distancing themselves from the Confederate dagger that had torn apart the Union center, thousands of fleeing Federals filled the countryside around them. Generals Crittenden and McCook were each fleeing the field as well, heading for the rear and safety.

While Rosecrans and Garfield rode to Rossville, the sounds of the continuing fight could be heard by the officers among their party. Garfield believed that the sounds of steady musket volleys were coming from Thomas, whose men were still holding the left of the Federal line. Rosecrans, whom Garfield later described as "abstracted," instead thought that all was lost and preferred to continue on to Chattanooga to reorganize and salvage what was left of the army. Garfield's description of Rosecrans at this time, given in private conversation with his friend Jacob Cox, has come under scrutiny by those wishing to defend Rosecrans, who instead argue that he was still fully in control at that point. However, Rosecrans himself later wrote to his brother that his retreat from the field that day "was possibly one of the most trying and anxious periods of my life." He acknowledged that he could hear "the swarming rebel host" continue to assault the remaining Federal positions. In the moment of crisis, as Rosecrans rode along, he relied on his rock-solid faith, reciting prayers and asking for God's assistance. Upon reaching Rossville, the party encountered scattered remnants of James Negley's division, which was supposed to have been on Thomas's left. Seeing Negley's men retreating, Rosecrans assumed Thomas had been routed as well.[205]

With the sounds of battle continuing, the commanding general and his chief of staff stopped to discuss the matter. As Garfield affirmed years later in a conversation with Henry Mills Alden, while Rosecrans was convinced that the army had been beaten, Garfield still maintained that Thomas was holding the Federal left flank intact and that it was imperative that someone ride to the Union left. Rosecrans and Garfield agreed that it was important for

Garfield's ride at Chickamauga, as depicted in an illustration in 1895.
McClure's Magazine.

the commanding general to continue to Chattanooga in order to reorganize the retreating forces there. Having been pressed by Garfield for permission to ride toward Thomas and the sound of battle, Rosecrans agreed, bidding his chief of staff farewell. Rosecrans proceeded on to Chattanooga to "receive and reorganize" the army, while Garfield was to ride back toward the battlefield. Having reached Rossville at around 2:00 p.m., Garfield now turned around, and with several staff officers accompanying him, the

Ride to Glory, by Amy Lindenberger, depicting Garfield's ride to Thomas at Chickamauga on September 20, 1863. *James A. Garfield National Historic Site.*

Ohioan spurred his horse to find the command of George Thomas. While the coming years would be filled with controversy regarding this moment, with questions over whether Garfield was ordered to Thomas and whether or not Rosecrans truly believed his army was defeated, the historical record makes one thing abundantly clear: while Union soldiers fought for their survival on the Federal left, it was James Garfield—not William Rosecrans—who rode toward the sound of battle that day.[206]

As Garfield set out, he was roughly six miles away from Thomas's position. It is not clear what exactly occurred during Garfield's famous ride because he never provided a thorough written account, though later biographers would greatly dramatize the event, making it a central feature of Garfield's war story in the 1880 presidential campaign. The party did come under enemy fire as it closed in on the Union lines, encountering Confederate skirmishers near the Cloud Church on La Fayette Road. The Confederate volleys forced Garfield and his party off the road when a bullet struck Garfield's horse, delivering a flesh wound. One of the riders accompanying Garfield was also hit, as was another of the horses. After encountering the enemy, Garfield's party closed in on the brigade of Colonel Dan McCook, where they finally reached the safety of Union lines. With his official report for the battle, McCook submitted a map indicating the spot where "General Garfield ran the gantlet [*sic*]" that afternoon. From McCook's lines, Garfield soon found Thomas, later writing, "I shall never forget my amazement and admiration when I beheld Thomas holding his own with utter defeat on each side and wild confusion in the rear."[207]

When Garfield arrived, the Federal lines were holding to a strong defensive position west of the La Fayette Road on Horseshoe Ridge and Snodgrass Hill. Thomas had made his headquarters at the Snodgrass Cabin, and it was there that Garfield met up with the 14th Corps commander. Thomas noted Garfield's arrival in his official report, stating that Garfield "reached this position about 4 pm., in company with Lt. Col. Thruston, of McCook's staff, and Captains Gaw and Barker, of my staff, who had been sent to the rear to bring back ammunition, if possible. General Garfield gave me the first reliable information that the right and center of our army had been driven, and of its condition at that time." Another observer, a correspondent from the *Cincinnati Gazette*, recorded the following dramatic account of Garfield's ride:

> *Just before the storm broke, the brave and high souled Garfield was perceived making his way to the headquarters of General Thomas. He had come to be present at the final contest, and in order to do so had ridden all the way from Chattanooga* [Garfield had instead ridden from Rossville], *passing through a fiery ordeal upon the road. His horse was shot under him, and his orderly was killed by his side. Still he had come through, he scarce knew how, and here he was to inspire fresh courage in the hearts of the brave soldiers who were holding the enemy at bay, to bring them words of greeting from General Rosecrans, and to inform them that the latter was reorganizing the scattered troops, and, as fast as possible, would hurry them forward to their relief.*

Garfield's arrival was the first chance for Thomas to learn what had happened to the center and right wing of the Union line. All through the afternoon, while Rosecrans and the rest of the army were falling back toward Tennessee, Thomas and his men held on with brute strength and determination. Indeed, George Thomas, soon to be known as "the Rock of Chickamauga," was the anchor protecting the rest of the Army of the Cumberland that day. For the rest of his life, Garfield maintained a deep respect for Thomas. He said of the general, "His character was as grand and simple as a colossal pillar of unchiseled granite."[208]

Among the battle-weary soldiers of Thomas's command, Garfield's presence was both noted and appreciated. Colonel Charles Harker, who commanded some of the same regiments that Garfield had led at Shiloh, included praise for Garfield in his official report, writing "that the presence of such tried and experienced officers as Major Generals Thomas and Gordon Granger and Brigadier Generals Wood and Garfield at the important position held by our troops, did much to inspire them with confidence during the eventful afternoon of the 20th." Major General Gordon Granger, commanding the reserve corps that he brought forward of his own accord to assist Thomas, also believed that Garfield's presence on the field was "animating and cheering both officers and men." Also

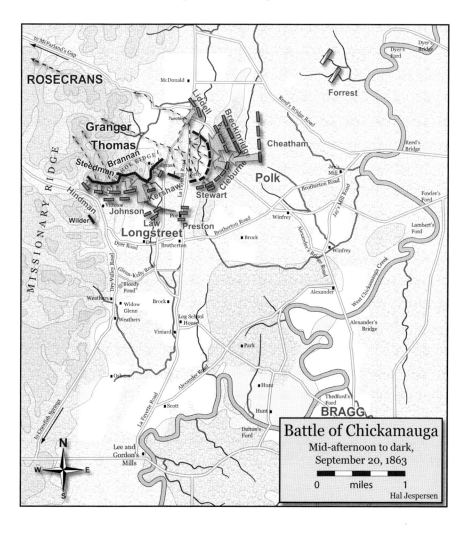

Battle of Chickamauga
Mid-afternoon to dark,
September 20, 1863
Hal Jespersen

among the battle-weary Union soldiers on Snodgrass Hill that day was William B. Hazen, Garfield's longtime friend from Hiram, Ohio, who was now a brigadier general in the army.[209]

Soon after reaching Thomas's position, Garfield fired off a quick dispatch to Rosecrans to apprise his commander of the situation on the field. Timed at 3:45 p.m., the message told Rosecrans that Thomas was still fighting with a sizable contingent of the army, "hold[ing] nearly all his old ground of this morning." Garfield believed Thomas was creating an opportunity for the army, rendering unnecessary any general retreat to Chattanooga. "The hardest fighting I have seen today is now going on here," he concluded, urging Rosecrans to come forward to Rossville with more ammunition for the army.[210]

Rosecrans himself was just then arriving in Chattanooga, disheartened and believing the situation was beyond repair. The commanding general was in an extremely fragile state. The long and tenuous campaign, with all of its stresses, along with a lack of enough sleep and the terrible events of that day had caught up with him. When he arrived at the headquarters of Brigadier General George Wagner, Rosecrans had difficulty dismounting his horse and needed help. According to Lieutenant Henry Cist, one of Rosecrans's staff officers, "He had the appearance of one broken in spirit… He had been in the saddle all day from before daylight, with nothing to eat since then. Rarely has mortal man been called on to undergo the terrible mental strain that had been on him during the week just past."[211]

In this condition, rather than waiting to hear from Garfield, Rosecrans sent orders to Thomas giving him command of all troops still on the field of battle and instructing him to withdraw from the field toward Rossville, where he was to "assume a threatening attitude." Having held his ground throughout the day, valiantly saving part—if not all—of the Army of the Cumberland, Thomas now had to abandon the hotly contested ground. Throughout the rest of the afternoon, Thomas's and Granger's men held on to their positions. Once darkness fell on the field, they fell back toward Rossville, and the Battle of Chickamauga came to a merciful end.[212]

That afternoon, while the right and center of the army faded away in the face of a withering Confederate onslaught, Thomas had held the Union left. While Rosecrans had made his way back to Chattanooga, it was to George Thomas and the sounds of battle that Garfield had ridden. When he arrived on Snodgrass Hill, Garfield witnessed one of the great sights of the American Civil War: Thomas's men fending off Confederate attacks for several hours with the fate of the Army of the Cumberland hanging in the balance. Thomas would live until 1870, accomplishing a great deal more during the war, but he would be forever known as the "Rock of Chickamauga" for his actions that afternoon. In 1870, Garfield eulogized Thomas with moving words at a reunion for the Society of the Army of the Cumberland. Of Thomas's stand that September afternoon seven years earlier, Garfield proclaimed, "He was, indeed, the 'Rock of Chickamauga,' against which the wild waves of battle dashed in vain. It will stand written forever in the annals of his country, that there he saved from destruction the Army of the Cumberland."[213]

That evening, having withdrawn with Thomas, Garfield sent another dispatch to Rosecrans at 8:40 p.m. Once again, Garfield informed Rosecrans of the army's position, providing a summary of Thomas's actions that day. Thomas, along with Granger's Reserve Corps, "fought a most terrific battle and has damaged the enemy badly." Garfield noted that time and again, Thomas and his men "successfully repelled the repeated combined attacks, most fiercely made, of the whole rebel army, frequently pressing the front and both flanks at the same time." In spite of the disaster that befell the Union right and center, Garfield believed that such brave and gallant fighting afforded the army an opportunity to salvage the situation. "The rebels have, however, done their best today, and I believe we can whip them tomorrow. I believe we can crown the whole battle with victory." He urged Rosecrans to come to Rossville in the morning to resume the fight. The dispatch finished, Garfield was exhausted. September 20, 1863, had been among the most eventful days of his life. That morning, Garfield had ridden the Union battle lines with Rosecrans, rightfully believing that they were well positioned for victory; that evening, Garfield and Rosecrans were miles apart—separated by the detritus of a defeated army—with the chief of staff trying to convince the commanding general to return to the front and continue the fight.[214]

On September 21, while Federal troops expected renewed attacks at Rossville, nothing but scattered skirmishing greeted the Army of the Cumberland. Shortly after midnight, Garfield again urged Rosecrans to act: "I hope you will get here as soon as possible to organize the army and victory before the storm sets in." By the time the sun rose, however, Garfield had abandoned his optimism of the night before, instead writing to Rosecrans that he was now unsure if the Federal lines were strong enough to hold; he indicated that he would soon be headed to Chattanooga to see the commander. Later that day, Rosecrans ordered Thomas to hold his lines until nightfall and then to withdraw back to Chattanooga.[215]

When Garfield arrived in Chattanooga on September 21, the situation facing the Army of the Cumberland was grim. While his messages from the front had an air of optimism, no such spirit was found at army headquarters. On the afternoon of September 20, soon after Garfield had sent his message indicating his arrival on Snodgrass Hill, Assistant Secretary of War Dana had sent a message to Washington proclaiming disaster. Despite the continued resistance of the Federal left, Dana believed all was lost, writing, "Chickamauga is as fatal a name in our history as Bull Run." About an hour later, at 5:00 p.m., just after Rosecrans received Garfield's message, the commanding general sent his own dispatch to Halleck telling of the "serious disaster" that had occurred.[216]

Rosecrans had good reason to be dispirited. He and his army had been through a trying ordeal. As Henry Cist wrote, "The Battle of Chickamauga was the hardest fought and bloodiest battle of the rebellion." Cist was partially correct; only Gettysburg had more overall casualties than Chickamauga. Still, the cost for both armies was enormous. Over thirty-four thousand casualties had fallen during the battle. The blood-soaked fields of Chickamauga had drained the army's strength and morale. The Confederates had gained their largest victory of the war in the western theater. Yet the campaign was not yet over.[217]

By September 22, the Army of the Cumberland had gathered itself at Chattanooga. All realized that the Confederate army was still nearby, and within days, the Army of Tennessee had closed in and managed to cut off most of the supplies coming into the city. On September 25, Garfield wrote home to Lucretia, using a positive spin to tell her of the battle and the army's condition:

> I will not attempt now, perhaps not till I see you, to give you a history of the battle which was much the fiercest we have had in the West, perhaps anywhere during the war. I will only say it was won and then abandoned, giving the enemy an opportunity to follow and injure us, but he was too much crippled to do so till we had strengthened ourselves in this place and were able to repulse all his attempts.[218]

That same day, Confederate artillery pieces began to fire down on the Federal camps from the mountains and ridges above the city. By the end of the month, the Army of the Cumberland was on reduced rations; hunger and desperation began to set in among the men. In the midst of this, urgent calls went out for reinforcements. Garfield himself sent one of them directly to Chase in Washington on September 23, stating, "We can stand here ten days, if help will then arrive. If we hold this point we shall save the campaign, even if we lose this army." With messages such as these, it was clear that help was needed for the Army of the Cumberland. In a bold move, two corps from the Army of the Potomac—totaling roughly twenty thousand men—were ordered to Chattanooga. It would take nine days and 1,159 miles to get there, but help was on the way for Rosecrans and his army.[219]

In early October, food became exasperatingly short for the Federals in Chattanooga. Many regiments were down to half rations, and the supplies coming in had ground to a halt. Having just been driven from the field at Chickamauga with a great cost in lives, now the survivors of that battle faced hunger, the soldiers' most persistent enemy. Many had suffered the defeat at Chickamauga well enough, still managing to cheer Rosecrans as he rode along Union lines on September 22. Now, as their haversacks were empty, so was their belief in their leader. Captain George Lewis of the 124th Ohio summed up what many were thinking when he wrote, "Never in the history of the Army of the Cumberland had the spirit of its officers and men been more depressed. The Battle of Chickamauga had not only been fought and lost, but we also lost what was more than losing a battle. We had lost confidence in our commander." Even with the arrival of reinforcements from the east, Rosecrans's army was barely hanging on. His support in Washington was completely gone. Several high-ranking cabinet members were openly lobbying for his removal.[220]

Knowing the odds against him, in mid-October, Rosecrans decided to send Garfield to Washington to report in person on the condition of the army. Rosecrans knew that his time with Garfield would soon be at an end regardless; within a few weeks, his chief of staff would be leaving to take his seat in the new Congress. Because Garfield was well connected in Washington, and because the two men had worked so closely together for so long, Rosecrans chose him to carry word of the army and its condition to the War Department. Before Garfield left, Rosecrans composed a glowing and complimentary thanks and goodbye to his chief of staff. On October 10, Rosecrans issued General Orders 231, which read as follows:

Brig. General James A. Garfield has been chosen by his fellow citizens to represent them in the councils of the nation. His high intelligence, spotless integrity, business capacity and thorough acquaintance with the wants of the Army, will render his service, if possible, more valuable to the country

in Congress than with us. Reluctantly yielding to this consideration, the
General commanding relieves him from duty as Chief of Staff. In doing so
he returns his thanks to General Garfield for the invaluable assistance he
has rendered him by wise councils and assiduous labors, as well as for his
gallantry, good judgment and efficiency at the Battle of Chickamauga.[221]

On October 15, Garfield received his last instructions from Rosecrans, ordering him to report on the army's conduct at Chickamauga, as well as "to see the Secretary of War and the General-in-Chief, and explain to them in detail our condition here…This must be gone into particularly; much depends on this condition of affairs."[222]

Having served with them for nine months, James Garfield left the soldiers of the Army of the Cumberland behind in mid-October 1863. He would forever be connected with the army and its commander, William Rosecrans, especially with the recent actions at Chickamauga. As he made his way north from the besieged city of Chattanooga, he was leaving his active military service in the field for the final time.

On October 16, the day after Garfield was ordered north and before he could deliver any news of Rosecrans and the army's predicament, President Lincoln held a fateful cabinet meeting in Washington. During the meeting, a decision was reached regarding the fate of the Union high command in the West. Lincoln's cabinet voted to relieve Rosecrans of command. Lincoln himself agreed, though he would not give the order himself. Instead, the Military Division of the Mississippi was created, with Major General Ulysses S. Grant placed in command of the primary armies operating in the war's western theater, including the departments of the Ohio, Tennessee and Cumberland. Grant was to head for Chattanooga himself to take command. The same orders giving Grant his command and directing him to proceed to Chattanooga also sealed the fate of Rosecrans. On October 19, after Edwin Stanton had personally delivered Grant his new orders, the general issued General Order No. 1, relieving William Rosecrans from his command of the Army of the Cumberland. George Thomas was to take his place.[223]

And thus it was that William Rosecrans was removed following the Battle of Chickamauga. Rosecrans was a good general who was done in by the complexities of his situation. He lacked the drive of Grant, showing it only in the Chickamauga Campaign when he responded to the prodding from Washington by moving his army forward perhaps too quickly and subjecting it to being torn apart in the bloodiest battle of the war's western theater. His career shows that even for good generals, victories were not easy to come by in the Civil War.

As Thomas took charge of the Army of the Cumberland, Garfield was headed to Washington, this time to stay. Indeed, when Garfield arrived at the capital in October 1863, it was the beginning of his tenure there that lasted throughout his congressional career and into his presidency in 1881. This moment marked a significant turning point for James Garfield. He set aside his uniform and said goodbye to the battlefields of the Civil War; for the rest of his life, Garfield would be a politician. His military career in the Union army had taken him to Kentucky, Tennessee, Mississippi, Alabama and Georgia. Along the way, he had fought in battles ranging from Middle Creek, with fewer than one hundred casualties, to helping oversee the Army of the Cumberland at the horrific Battle of Chickamauga. He made political friends and allies who would support his political career and his ambitions for the rest of his life. His path had crossed with those of Lincoln, Grant, Sherman, Thomas, Rosecrans, Halleck and many others, all of whom influenced Garfield along the way. Without his service during the war, James Garfield never would have enjoyed the postwar political career that he did. His status as a leading Republican in the later 1860s and 1870s was based on his military record above all else. He was not someone who sought out the presidency, certainly not in 1863, but his actions in the army are what made all of his postwar success possible.

When Garfield entered Congress, he was thirty-two years old, just one year shy of the age of his father, Abram Garfield, when he died in the old Western Reserve in 1833. James was not yet two at the time. He was left without a father and grew up in dire poverty. That he worked his way through life to become a college president, state senator and general was a remarkable testament both to his perseverance and the possibilities available to a young man in the United States. In a war dominated by generals who were educated at West Point, Garfield was a self-taught man who rose to his rank through hard work. His rise was only possible in the Union for which he fought during the Civil War. In his congressional career, he continued to fight for the same ideals and principles that enabled him to rise from a log cabin to the highest levels of the Union army during the war.

Before he took his seat in Congress in December, Garfield was busied with numerous tasks and responsibilities. He stopped home briefly to meet his new son—Harry Augustus Garfield—who was born while Garfield was away at war. He met with Stanton and Lincoln and carried out his task of speaking with them and telling them of the Battle of Chickamauga. He even had time to take part in political campaigning, delivering several speeches to abolitionist rallies in Maryland.[224]

Yet before he began his congressional career, Garfield—who had seen so much suffering already in 1863 on the battlefield—experienced a tragic loss of his own. On December 1, his daughter Eliza, whom he affectionately called "Trot," died in Hiram a few months short of her fourth birthday. Garfield mentioned Trot lovingly in nearly every letter home from the war. Just before departing Chattanooga, he closed his letter to Lucretia, "Kiss little Trot for me a dozen times. I am very anxious to see the little rascal."[225]

Having buried his firstborn child, Garfield left home for Washington, D.C. On December 5, 1863, he officially resigned from the United States Army, leaving at the rank of major general, a rank he was awarded for his bravery at Chickamauga, dating to September 19, 1863, eighteen years to the day before his death at the hands of an assassin.[226]

Just days after resigning from the army, in a letter to his dear friend Captain Swaim, Garfield wrote movingly of the loss of his child while he looked ahead—regretfully, it seems—to the next chapter of his life.

The first found me at the bedside of my precious little girl. She died December 1st and was buried December 3rd. I left early the following morning for this place. I have no words to tell how very desolate my life has seemed since the light of her little life went out…I try to be cheerful and plunge into the whirlpool of work which opens before me…

I need not tell you how great the struggle is for me to stay away from the army in its glorious career, but I shall try to do cheerfully what seems to be a duty.[227]

CHAPTER 9
Veteran

DECEMBER 1863–SEPTEMBER 1881

It is hard to grasp in an hour the grand parabolic picture of these eventful years.
—James A. Garfield

When General James Garfield resigned from the army in December 1863, the Civil War was far from over. Yet for the final year and a half of combat, Garfield took his battles to the halls of Congress, delivering his characteristically eloquent, poignant and emotional speeches in favor of the Union war effort. The same devotion to the Union that he had displayed on the battlefield was now manifested in his congressional career. When he left the Ohio State Senate in 1861, he was among the first to have realized the potential impact of the war. From the day he heard of the shots fired on Fort Sumter, Garfield believed that the Union could be preserved only at a great cost of blood and treasure, a price he was willing to pay. In April 1861, he stated that he would rather lose one million men in battle than see the Confederacy succeed and the Union be torn apart. He carried that conviction with him through the war, clashing with moderates and those who sought a more amicable resolution. His wartime experience only deepened his belief in the righteousness of the Union cause and of the sinfulness of slavery. Garfield's abolitionist sentiments blossomed further on the battlefield, and when he entered Congress, he fought for them just as fiercely, now using speeches and resolutions as his weapons of choice. The voice he added to the discussion of how to prosecute the war was one tempered by the war itself. His opinions were those of one who had fought Confederate armies in Kentucky, Tennessee and Georgia. His experience was from the fields of Middle Creek, Shiloh and Chickamauga.

As a war veteran and a Republican, James Garfield was a valuable member of the new Congress. Despite his youthful age and his lack of congressional experience, Garfield made his presence felt early on in his congressional career. As a Portage County newspaper described, the young congressman from Ohio stood out from the rest: "Garfield's voice is heard. Every ear attends…his eloquent words move the heart, convince the reason, and tell the weak and wavering which way to go." He possessed an element of political courage, being willing to go against the leaders of his own party on issues such as providing bounties for new enlistees, something he worried would be costly for the government.[228]

In late January 1864, Garfield made his first major appearance on the House floor. If he was not already known as a radical congressman before the speech, he certainly cemented his reputation as such with his remarks. His speech was on the question of what to do about confiscating Confederate property. Garfield came down firmly on the side of complete and unforgiving punishment of those aiding the rebellion, believing that the best way to win the war and secure a better Union was to wipe away the Southern slaveholding system with complete destruction. He stated that the Union army in the field was clearly now "an abolition army," and only might and power could bring the war to a close and finish off the Confederacy:

> *I tell you, gentlemen, the heart of this great rebellion cannot be softened by smiles. You cannot send commissioners to Richmond…to smile away the horrible facts of this war. Not by smiles, but by thundering volleys, must this rebellion be met, and by such means alone…*
>
> *Mr. Speaker, if we want a peace that is not a hollow peace, we must follow that example, and make thorough work of this war. We must establish freedom in the midst of servitude, and the authority of law in the midst of rebellion.*

In a powerful reference, Garfield compared the sins of the Confederacy in rebelling against the Union to the sins of Satan when he rebelled against God in Heaven: "Let the republic drive from its soil the traitors that have conspired against its life, as God and his angels drove Satan and his host from heaven."[229]

Serving on the Military Affairs Committee, headed by Representative Robert Schenk, himself a former general with whom Garfield was boarding at the time, Garfield was involved in the measures relating to the war itself, a fitting role for someone who just a few months before was in the army. The year 1864 portended to be the bloodiest one of the war, and as such, new recruits were needed to fill the holes in the ranks of the Union army. Garfield and his committee tried to push through a new conscription bill, authorizing the drafting of thousands of new Federal troops. Garfield argued in favor of the measure in front of the House in late June, delivering a forceful speech supporting the draft. He condemned the idea of commutation, a process that allowed individuals simply to buy their way out of serving. With strong radical support, the bill continuing the draft passed on July 4, 1864, and commutation was not a part of it.[230]

As 1864 continued, Garfield gained valuable experience in the halls of Congress, forming the basis for the rest of his political career. As a radical Republican, he often grew frustrated with President Lincoln, believing him to be too cautious in prosecuting the war, lacking the strong-handed approach that Garfield preferred. He had fully supported Lincoln in 1860, but now, after hundreds of thousands had died in the war, Garfield believed harsher measures were needed to put down the rebellion. While he believed Lincoln was not perhaps the best candidate for reelection in 1864—"the Administration is not all I could wish," he wrote early that year—he knew that it would be wise to back the sitting president. While some moved to have Garfield's friend Salmon Chase run for the presidency, Garfield thought better of it, knowing that many in Ohio, as well as the vast majority of the soldiers in the army, strongly favored the president.[231]

Despite his tepid support of the president, Garfield was re-nominated by the Nineteenth Congressional District in 1864, and that fall he won his reelection to Congress by a margin of nearly three to one. Lincoln himself won a second term as well, defeating the Democratic Party contender, George B. McClellan. Garfield had long disliked McClellan, seeing him as a West Point general who did not properly understand the war or possess the necessary skill to defeat the Confederacy. His letters of 1862 were filled with denunciations of McClellan, especially during Garfield's time in Washington and the Fitz John Porter court-martial. While Garfield was not enthusiastic about Lincoln, he certainly preferred him to McClellan.

In January 1865, as the war was entering its final months, the defining issue of freedom in the United States was taking center stage in Congress, and Garfield was playing his role in fighting for liberty. In 1864, the U.S. Senate passed a draft of the Thirteenth Amendment to the United States Constitution, the language of which forever abolished slavery in the United

States. The amendment had lacked political support in the U.S. House of Representatives, but following the 1864 elections, a renewed push was made to pass the measure through the lame duck Congress before the end of the war. While Republicans worked behind the scenes to pass the amendment, Garfield himself took to the floor to deliver one of the most passionate and impressive speeches of his life. "We shall never know why slavery dies so hard in this republic and in this hall till we know why sin has such longevity and Satan is immortal," Garfield began. He pointed out that after all the blood that had been shed and all the sacrifices that had been made, the fate of slavery lay before them. The institution was suffering from mortal wounds, and it was in the hands of Congress, Garfield argued, to deliver the final deathblow. He proceeded in making a lengthy and detailed case answering the critics of the amendment, ensuring that it was a just and righteous measure, one that was necessary for the nation. After it passed the House on January 31, 1865—Garfield voted yes, of course—the measure was signed by Lincoln, a man whom Garfield had grown to respect, even if he did not believe that Lincoln always went as far on radical policies as Garfield and other Republicans desired.[232]

Within a few months of the Thirteenth Amendment's passage, the war finally and mercifully came to an end. On April 9, 1865, Robert E. Lee surrendered his Army of Northern Virginia to Ulysses S. Grant at Appomattox, and in the coming weeks, thousands more Confederates stacked their arms and surrendered to Federal troops. The end of the fighting meant that a new era in American history had begun; now the nation would need to rebuild itself. Yet it would do so without the man who had led the country through its fiery trial, the man whom Garfield had first met in February 1861 when he was traveling through Ohio on his way to Washington to take the oath of office as the sixteenth president. On the fateful day of April 15, 1865, Garfield was in New York attending to matters of business. Much like the rest of the nation, he was shattered by the news of Abraham Lincoln's assassination, the first time in American history that a president had been killed by an assassin's bullet. Writing to Lucretia, he expressed his deep sorrow for the nation's loss:

> *My heart is so broken with our great national loss that I can hardly think or write or speak. I reached here Friday night at midnight and in the morning heard the shocking news…Places of business have been closed. Nothing is in the heart of anyone but great sorrow…The day is nearly gone and I have as yet done nothing. I am sick at heart and feel it to be almost like a sacrilege to talk of money or business now.*[233]

While Garfield had not always appreciated Lincoln, like the country at large, he grew to revere him following his death. On April 14, 1866, one year after the president's assassination, Garfield delivered a moving eulogy, calling for the House to adjourn out of respect for the slain president. Garfield believed that the assassination of the president was "an event unparalleled in the history of nations, certainly unparalleled in our own":

> *The last five years have been marked by wonderful developments of individual character. Thousands of our people, before unknown to fame, have taken their places in history, crowned with immortal honors. In thousands of humble homes are dwelling heroes and patriots whose names shall never die. But greatest among all these great developments were the character and fame of Abraham Lincoln whose loss the nation still deplores.*[234]

Garfield's moving tribute to Lincoln both described the slain president and, unknowingly, himself, a future president. His name was among those that had risen to fame and taken its place in history during the previous years of the rebellion. His status in the army afforded him a position from which he eventually rose to the presidency himself, only to tragically join Lincoln as a leader felled by an assassin.

Over the next fourteen years, James Garfield remained a congressman from Ohio. He rose in importance in Congress, serving on numerous committees. He strongly supported the gold standard and opposed paper money, advocating for free trade instead of protective tariffs. By the mid-1870s, he was one of the most influential and important Republicans in the House of Representatives. Throughout that decade, as numerous Republicans made runs at the presidency, Garfield sat quietly by, displaying humility and reservations at seeking any higher office. Of the idea that he might one day get the "presidential fever," Garfield wrote in his journal in early 1879, "I am determined it shall not seize me…In almost ever[y] case it impairs if it does not destroy the usefulness of its victim."[235]

Garfield's refusal to participate in presidential politics held out until the summer of 1880. The Republicans were meeting in Chicago for their nominating convention that year, just as they had twenty years before when Lincoln had become the surprise nominee. Indeed, just as in 1860, the 1880 Republican Convention had numerous men jockeying for the presidential nomination. Garfield—who at the time was a senator-elect thanks to the Republican legislature in Ohio—was a supporter of fellow Ohioan John Sherman as a candidate. He even delivered a speech expressing his support

Garfield's life story was featured in numerous publications during his political career. *Library of Congress.*

on Sherman's behalf. Yet as the balloting process began, the convention delegates found themselves at an impasse. Of the front-runners, including James Blaine, John Sherman and Ulysses S. Grant, none was successful. Soon, a new name was added: that of James A. Garfield. By the thirty-sixth ballot, in spite of protests from Garfield, the verdict of the convention was clear. James A. Garfield was the Republican nominee for president.

After the nominating convention in June, Garfield's life would never be the same. The coming months saw him engaged in a "front porch campaign," where thousands traveled to his home in Mentor, Ohio, to hear him speak.

JAMES A. GARFIELD
REPUBLICAN CANDIDATE FOR PRESIDENT

CHESTER A. ARTHUR
REPUBLICAN CANDIDATE FOR VICE PRESIDENT

The 1880 Republican candidates for president and vice president. *Library of Congress.*

Garfield's oratory was persuasive, and those actively campaigning on his behalf across the country were as well. Though the Democrats also nominated a Civil War general, Winfield Hancock of Pennsylvania, Garfield ultimately prevailed. The popular vote was narrowly in Garfield's favor, but the Republicans had a solid victory in the Electoral College. On November 2, 1880, James Garfield was elected the twentieth president of the United States. Nine months later, to the exact day, President Garfield was shot in a train station in Washington, D.C., dying of his wounds a few months after.

"THE YEARS HAVE PASSED... THE REPUBLIC LIVES"

For the rest of his life, until he followed Lincoln to the grave as a victim of assassination, the Civil War was a constant presence and of the utmost importance for James Garfield. Of all the positions he held during his life— teacher, minister, college president, state senator, congressman, presidential nominee and president of the United States—perhaps none was as meaningful to James Garfield as the simple title of "General Garfield." His military service helped to define the rest of his life. It was not as a private citizen that Garfield became a key and leading Republican in Congress and later a presidential candidate. It was as a Civil War veteran.

As a veteran, Garfield maintained relationships with many of those with whom he had fought during the war. His military service not only brought him into the midst of some of the most eventful moments of the war, but it also brought him in contact with other future leaders of the United States. Even within his own 42nd Ohio, there were several officers of future distinction. When Garfield left the 42nd in March 1862, Lionel Sheldon rose to the rank of full colonel, achieving a distinguished Civil War career in his own right. After the war, Sheldon practiced law in New Orleans and was elected to Congress for three terms, serving with Garfield as a Republican in the U.S. House of Representatives. From 1881 to 1885, Sheldon was the governor of the New Mexico Territory. He lived until 1917, when he died in Pasadena, California. Major Don Pardee, who led Union soldiers up the wooded slopes around Middle Creek in January 1862, was promoted to lieutenant colonel in March 1862, ultimately taking command of the regiment later on in the war. When the war ended, Pardee also became an attorney in New Orleans, later becoming a judge and running for state attorney general. Because of his judicial experience and their military connection, Garfield nominated Pardee to the U.S. Fifth Circuit Court just ten days after he became president in 1881. Pardee would serve as a federal judge for thirty-eight years, the longest of any of Garfield's judicial appointments.

In addition to Sheldon and Pardee, Garfield's close friend Jacob Cox became a prominent figure after the war as well. Cox was elected the governor of Ohio, serving from 1866 to 1868. When Ulysses S. Grant was elected president, Cox became the secretary of the interior, serving for several years in the Grant administration. In the late 1870s, he, too, was elected to Congress, also serving alongside Garfield in the House of Representatives. Throughout the rest of his life, Garfield maintained connections with the officers with whom he had served, continuing their bonds of friendship that had been forged years before in the war.

Garfield never lost sight of the causes for which the war had been fought. With the end of the war came the beginning of Reconstruction, as murky and muddied as any era in American history. Garfield's political ascendancy during this time was entirely from within Congress. Questions arose about how Congress and the nation could guarantee African

James A. Garfield during the 1870s, when he was a member of the U.S. House of Representatives. *Library of Congress.*

Americans the new civil rights that they had won at the close of the war. New amendments were passed abolishing slavery, guaranteeing the federal protection of rights and allowing African Americans to vote, all of which were supported by Garfield. While Garfield worked to pass such amendments, he still maintained a personal unease with social advances made by African Americans, something that was common for even the most radical supporters of civil rights during Reconstruction.

While Garfield was stronger than most in speaking out in favor of civil rights for freed African Americans, he is part of the particular tragedy of

Reconstruction. Having won the war for the Union and abolished slavery, the Reconstruction-era presidents—most all of whom had fought in the war—failed to carry through and secure the promises of the freedom for which they had fought. Each president encountered his own difficulties in accomplishing these goals. Rutherford Hayes, for example, was elected only after a narrow and hotly contested election that saw concessions made to the South regarding the removal of federal troops, effectively ending Reconstruction and hamstringing Hayes's abilities to enforce civil rights in the South.

Garfield was limited by a much more obvious reason: his shockingly short presidency. He was in office and healthy for only four months, giving him little time for major accomplishments in any arena, let alone the complicated field of civil rights. In the time he had, Garfield appointed African Americans to positions within the federal government, including making Frederick Douglass the recorder of deeds in Washington, D.C. Garfield believed strongly that a federally backed education system in the South would be the key to helping to lift African Americans from poverty and degradation. Part of the tragedy of his assassination is that history never had the chance to see how these policies and reforms would emerge during a full Garfield presidency.

Nonetheless, Garfield certainly did carry the issues and legacy of the war with him to the presidency. In the campaign of 1880, he was nominated by Republicans over another war hero, Ulysses S. Grant, the same man whose name had appeared next to Garfield's in the thankful resolution of the Kentucky legislature eighteen years before. In the general election that fall, Garfield was running against Winfield Hancock, who rose to fame through leading the Union Second Corps at Gettysburg in 1863. During the 1880 campaign, Republicans and campaign biographers mined Garfield's Civil War career for stories of heroism. They took his famous ride at Chickamauga and made it a larger-than-life event, equating it with the very salvation of the country itself. Campaign marches and songs were written revolving around his heroic conduct during the war. During his famed "front porch campaign," as thousands came to Mentor, Ohio, to see the president at his home, many came to learn about the candidate for president who was affectionately known not as "Congressman Garfield" but "General Garfield," as he was referred to in news reports and campaign correspondence. During that campaign, he spoke at several dedication ceremonies for soldiers' monuments in the northeast Ohio area. At one such speech in Painesville that July, Garfield stated that monuments to those who fell during the war would stand for all time to tell future generations of the type of country their ancestors had struggled to preserve:

> *More than the bugler on the field, from his granite lips will go out a call that the children of Lake County will hear after the grave has covered us all and our immediate children. That is the teaching of your monument; that is its lesson. It is the lesson of endurance for what we believe. It is the lesson of sacrifice for what we love; the lesson of heroism for what we mean to sustain; and that lesson cannot be lost on a people like this.*[236]

Even Garfield's own running mate in 1880 had a Civil War connection. Though he did not see field service during the war, Chester A. Arthur of New York had been an officer with the New York State Quartermaster Department from 1861 to 1863, losing his position due to the election of Democratic governor Horatio Seymour halfway through the war.

In his inaugural address on March 4, 1881—twenty years to the day from when Lincoln took his oath of office—Garfield spoke movingly of the American past, noting that in the history of the United States, at no point had the country and its government been tested more than in the recent Civil War. "We ourselves are witnesses that the Union emerged from the blood and fire of that conflict purified and made stronger for all the beneficent purposes of good government," Garfield proclaimed. He stated that no political change in American history—save the founding of the nation—had been as important as the abolition of slavery, adding, "It has added immensely to the moral and industrial forces of our people."[237]

There were even Civil War connections to Garfield's untimely death. Among those who attended to him at the train station that fateful July day in 1881 was Robert Lincoln. In addition to being Garfield's secretary of war, Robert Lincoln was the son of the sixteenth president, and just sixteen years before, he had seen his own father become the first president to die as a result of assassination. After Garfield was shot, Robert Lincoln called for Dr. D.W. Bliss to come quickly and attend to the wounded president. Bliss had been a regimental surgeon with the 3rd Michigan Infantry during the Civil War, and in 1865, he was the head of the Army Square Hospital in Washington. When Lincoln was shot, Bliss had been one of those who had tried in vain to save the president's life. Now, he was called upon to save another president, one whose life was also forever changed by the Civil War.

After his months of prolonged suffering and sickness, when Garfield finally succumbed to his wounds in Elberon, New Jersey, his last words were spoken not to Lucretia, his children or Dr. Bliss but to David Swaim, the same man whom Garfield had met in 1862 while in the army. When Garfield was in command of the 20th Brigade that spring and summer, he chose Swaim, a member of the 65th Ohio Infantry, to serve on his staff. Garfield and Swaim established a close relationship, writing many letters to each other through the years. Indeed, it was to Swaim that Garfield had written that the summer of 1862 was a moment as difficult in history as Valley Forge had been during the Revolution. Before Garfield slipped into unconsciousness, at 10:00 p.m. on the evening of September 19, 1881, he complained to Swaim of a pain in his chest, closed his eyes and died half an hour later. Garfield passed away eighteen years to the day, and almost to the exact hour, from when he had been at the Widow Glenn's cabin at Chickamauga at a council of war with the commanders of the Army of the Cumberland.[238]

Garfield's body was brought from New Jersey to Washington, where he was laid in the Capitol Rotunda. Sixteen years after the first presidential assassination in American history, grief once again gripped the nation. A funeral train, adorned with black bunting to mourn the slain leader, once more bore the body of an assassinated president westward, though this time, the train went no farther than Cleveland. Garfield was interred in Lake View Cemetery, and in 1890, a massive memorial was finished to house his remains. When the monument was dedicated on Memorial Day of that year, massive crowds and dignitaries came to pay their respects to the slain president. Present were 115 veterans of the 42nd Ohio, there to honor their former commander. They marched with their old battle flags from the war at the head of a procession to the cemetery that day. President Benjamin Harrison was there for the occasion, as were former president Rutherford B. Hayes and future president William McKinley, all three of whom were Union veterans. Other attendees included John Schofield, the general of the army, as well as William Tecumseh Sherman. In the remarks delivered that day, the speakers frequently recapped Garfield's life accomplishments, lingering on his service to the Union during the war. His military career, as Ohio governor James Campbell noted, placed the martyred president among "the imperishable galaxy of men that Ohio furnished to the country between 1861 and 1865." With all the dignitaries that day, the honor of delivering the main oration went to a man who knew Garfield better than most, going back all the way to their days together in the Ohio Statehouse in 1860. Jacob Cox spoke at length about Garfield's life and character. Of Garfield's Civil War career, Cox spoke of the concept of duty and obligation to one's country, something that was so central to Garfield's life story:

The Garfield Memorial, where James and Lucretia are buried in Lake View Cemetery, Cleveland, Ohio. *Author's photo*.

"Garfield's path of duty again opened plainly before him, and he promptly stepped into it. All other obligations dwindled before the overmastering one of saving the national life." Thus, even at the dedication of his final resting place in Lake View Cemetery, Garfield's war record was a primary focus of those who remembered him.[239]

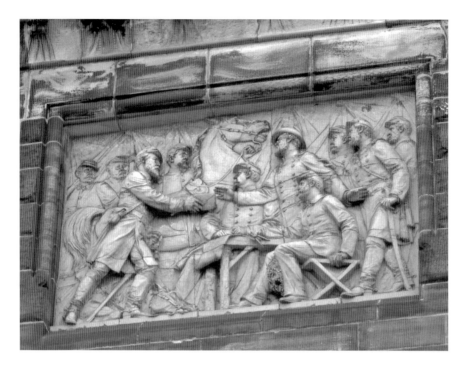

The exterior of the Garfield Memorial in Lake View Cemetery features numerous engravings covering Garfield's life. Pictured here is a scene representing his service with the Army of the Cumberland at Chickamauga, found on the front of the memorial. *Author's photo.*

Garfield was certainly not alone in having the war follow him for the rest of his life. It is common for those who have seen combat to be indelibly changed by the experience. The broad narrative of history shows this to be true time and again. After the war, Garfield related the story of his first sight of dead soldiers on the battlefield and the impact the scene had on him. Following the fight at Middle Creek in January 1862, he came upon several lifeless bodies of Confederates appearing as still as if the men had been asleep. Garfield remarked that, upon seeing the dead of the battlefield, "something went out of him, the habit of his lifetime, that never came back again; the sense of the sacredness of life and the impossibility of destroying it." In this regard, while his postwar political career led him to extraordinary heights, he was in many ways still an ordinary veteran.[240]

For as long as veterans lived after the Civil War, they met together in reunions and commemorative events to remember their wartime experiences. Garfield himself was able to attend many such gatherings, often delivering remarks to groups relating the importance of the war. As a congressman, he was a sought-after speaker at such events because of his eloquence and his military career. In his speeches about the war, Garfield always maintained the utmost reverence for those who suffered more than he did during the conflict. Other than experiencing severe sickness on numerous occasions, Garfield had survived the war unscathed. As a result, his feeling of indebtedness to those who served and suffered ran deep.

In 1879, one year before he was elected president, Garfield delivered remarks to a reunion of Union veterans who had survived being imprisoned at Andersonville, the infamous Confederate prison camp in Georgia. Garfield's speech displayed several of his basic beliefs on the meaning of the war. He spoke of sacrifice and the moral meaning of the conflict, as well as the importance of moving on as one united country. He began by acknowledging that he was somewhat uncomfortable at the gathering: "I have addressed a great many audiences, but I never before stood in the presence of one that I felt so wholly unworthy to speak to. A man who came through the war without being shot or made a prisoner, is almost out of place in such an assemblage as this." He spoke of the sacrifices made by those who were held in Confederate prisons, praising their willingness not only to fight for their country but also to starve, suffer and die in miserable conditions for it. Praising their patriotism, determination and courage, Garfield spoke of the higher ideals for which they and so many others had fought:

> *Who have reunions? I will not trench upon forbidden ground, but let me say this: Nothing on the earth and under the sky can call men together for reunions except ideas that have immortal truth and immortal life in them. The animals fight. Lions and tigers fight as ferociously as did you. Wild beasts tear to the death, but they never have reunions. Why? Because wild beasts do not fight for ideas. They merely fight for blood. All these men and all their comrades went out inspired by two immortal ideas: first, that liberty shall be universal in America; and second, that this old flag is the flag of a Nation, and not of a State—that the Nation is supreme over all people and all corporations. Call it a State; call it a section; call it a South; call it a North; call it anything you wish, and yet, armed with the nationality that God gave us, this is a Nation against all State sovereignty and secession whatever! It is the immortality of that truth that makes these reunions, and that makes this one. You believed it on the battle-field, you believed it in the hell of Andersonville, and you believe it to-day, thank God! and you will believe it to the last gasp...*

> *Finally, and in conclusion, I am willing, and I think that I speak for thousands of others—I am willing to see all the bitterness of the late war buried in the grave of our dead. I would be willing that we should imitate the condescending, loving kindness of Him who planted the green grass on the battle-fields and let the fresh flowers bloom on all the graves alike. I would clasp hands with those who fought against us, make them my brethren and forgive all the past, only on one supreme condition: that it be admitted in practice, acknowledged in theory, that the cause for which we fought and you suffered, was and is and forever more will be right, eternally right. That the cause for which they fought, was and forever will be the cause of treason and wrong. Until that is acknowledged, my hand shall never grasp any rebel's hand across any chasm, however small.*[241]

James Abram Garfield was a man made both by and for the Civil War. His life story, rising from the poverty of a log cabin to the presidency, was only possible in the Union that he and so many others fought to save. He was a volunteer soldier and officer in a volunteer war. His story is in many ways the story of the Union. Though not perfect, he came from the most humble beginnings, and through the fiery trial of the Civil War he rose to a position of leadership in a bold new era of American history. The war saw James Garfield go from the role of a college instructor and state legislator to the halls of the United States House of Representatives, the platform on which he would eventually prove himself worthy of the presidency. The men who emerged as leaders of the United States in the decades after the Civil War were those who largely achieved their roles because of what they had done for their country during that conflict. Just as the war transformed the United States, it transformed the lives of those who lived it, endured it and experienced it as well.

Garfield's life had both heroism and tragedy. While his presidency was cut tragically short by his assassination, the manner in which he served his country during the Civil War displayed the heroism that allowed him to reach the highest office in the land. Certainly, Garfield's military career was not perfect; he had his trials and tribulations and was caught up in some of the war's most trying hours. Garfield's role in the Fitz John Porter court-martial and his frustrations with Rosecrans in 1863 show his human side in the midst of war. Yet these imperfections do not detract from Garfield's Civil War record. They only remind us that all of our heroes, whether they be soldiers, generals or presidents, are just like us—still heroic in their service and sacrifice no matter the difficulties and obstacles they may

While Garfield held many titles in life, none was more meaningful to him than "General Garfield." *Library of Congress.*

encounter. When his country needed him most, James Garfield stepped forward. The manner in which he lifted himself up through hard work and serving his country during the Civil War ultimately led him to the highest office in the land.

Several months after Lincoln's death, in the summer of 1865, Garfield found himself in a familiar place once again. He was delivering an Independence Day oration in Ravenna, Ohio, where he had spoken on the same topic exactly five years before. The years between these two speeches had been some of the most trying and momentous times in American history. Hundreds of thousands had died, four million slaves had been freed and the nation had been fundamentally changed, experiencing "a new birth of freedom," as the recently martyred Lincoln had so eloquently declared in his famed Gettysburg Address. Just as the country had changed, Garfield had changed as well. Lucretia had given birth to two children, one of whom would live to adulthood. He was elected to Congress in 1862, emerging as a national political leader. He had joined the army, achieved the rank of major general of volunteers, led men in combat and served as the chief of staff for Union forces at one of the bloodiest battles in American history. The man who stood before the crowd in Ravenna in 1860 had predicted that the nation would never tear apart, likening the dissolution of the Union to splitting the waters of the Mississippi River. Now, in 1865, Garfield's speech

James A. Garfield, twentieth president of the United States. *Library of Congress.*

reflected the maturity he had gained, as well as the scars the nation still bore from the bloody fight to secure its continued existence:

> *It is hard to grasp in an hour the grand parabolic picture of these eventful years. Five years ago the Declaration of Independence was read and the orator used it as a base for his address. Since then the great documents that have just been read to us have been added to the wealth of the nation. We should be untrue to history, untrue to the Republic if we kept them all out of sight, and failed to give them place as they have given us hope, strength, and victory. Five years ago, we did not know that we had a Declaration, a country, or liberty. The years have passed. We have a country. The Republic lives, and today, with some reclamation of its greatness and goodness and power we have the privilege to glorify it before God.*[242]

The Republic that Garfield spoke of that day in Ravenna was vastly different from the nation he had discussed five years before in 1860. So, too, was James Garfield. The war had changed him, as well as the nation that he would one day be elected to lead.

The Garfield-Rosecrans Controversy

No aspect of James Garfield's Civil War career has had more lingering controversy than his relationship with William Rosecrans. The manner in which Garfield dealt with Rosecrans—especially in relation to the Battle of Chickamauga and its aftermath—has raised questions regarding what role Garfield played in the dismissal of his commanding general. In order to address the removal of Rosecrans—and Garfield's possible role in it— it is necessary to reevaluate the time frame in which the event occurred. The Battle of Chickamauga began late in the day on September 18 and concluded on September 20. By September 22, the Army of the Cumberland had retreated back into the confines of Chattanooga. The Union army's advance into Georgia had been stymied, and Union forces had sustained a major setback. By the start of October, the army's supplies had been virtually cut off by the Army of Tennessee. On October 15, under orders from Rosecrans, Garfield left Chattanooga, making his way north to speak with Stanton and Lincoln concerning the state of the army. The following day, Lincoln and his cabinet agreed to create the Military Division of the Mississippi, giving Ulysses S. Grant command of all Union troops between the Mississippi River and the Appalachian Mountains. Three days later, on October 19, Grant issued orders removing Rosecrans from command, just days before he arrived in Chattanooga to take control of the situation. While Garfield had a complex relationship with Rosecrans, at no point in between Chickamauga and Rosecrans's dismissal did he openly lobby for his commander's removal.[243]

APPENDIX A

Much of the controversy regarding Garfield's relationship with Rosecrans relates to the letters that he sent to Salmon Chase in Washington throughout 1863. Perhaps the most quoted of these letters was dated July 27, when Garfield vented his frustrations regarding the lack of offensive movements that had plagued the Army of the Cumberland that summer. As was noted in Chapter 8, this letter contains both praise and criticism of Rosecrans, assuming the form not of a treacherous missive but of a personal letter expressing frustrations with the slow pace of war in 1863. Certainly, Garfield had his doubts about Rosecrans and was far from offering him his unwavering support. Though this letter was written in July, it still became part of the conversation regarding Rosecrans's dismissal after Chickamauga.

On December 24, 1863, journalist James Gilmore attended a dinner party with Chase, where he and the secretary of the treasury discussed the matter of Rosecrans's removal from command. Chase informed Gilmore that the general had been removed because he had lost his wits at Chickamauga, becoming "totally unfitted to command." Chase claimed to have learned of this through a letter from a high-ranking official in the Union army at the battle, "Rosecrans's professed friend and admirer, James A. Garfield." Chase said that he had read this letter to Lincoln and the cabinet and that Garfield had therefore played a role in Rosecrans's dismissal following Chickamauga. Gilmore was stunned by this revelation. He had spoken with Garfield about Rosecrans the previous day without hearing of any such negative reports regarding the former commander of the Army of the Cumberland.[244]

Complicating matters further, in 1879, Charles Dana published a statement also claiming that Garfield had written a letter to Chase after Chickamauga that spoke poorly of Rosecrans's conduct and that it was that letter from the chief of staff that had "broke the camels' back" and convinced Lincoln to remove the general. Garfield flatly denied the accusation, telling Rosecrans that "any charge, whether it comes from Dana, or any other liar, to the effect that I was in any sense untrue to you or unfaithful to our friendship, has no particle of truth in it." Garfield stated that if it were true, whoever had the letter should come forward and publish it publicly.[245]

Three years later, once Garfield had been assassinated, Dana went ahead and published a letter that Garfield had written. However, it was not a letter that had been sent after Chickamauga; instead, he published the July 27, 1863 letter that Garfield had written to Chase. After Chase died in 1873, the letter was in the hands of his secretary, J.W. Shuckers, who gave it to

Appendix A

Dana in 1882. Dana then published the letter in the *New York Sun*, using it to unfairly accuse Garfield of treachery. Clearly, this letter had nothing to do with telling the Lincoln administration of Rosecrans's alleged failures at Chickamauga; it had been written nearly two months before the battle. Dana had waited until Garfield could no longer respond to publish the letter as evidence of his duplicity. Even though this letter was written before Chickamauga, Rosecrans was stunned. For the first time, he believed that Garfield had double-crossed him and contributed to his demise.

Certainly, as Chase and Dana claimed, there had been negative reports sent to Washington in October 1863 alleging that disaster would befall the Army of the Cumberland unless Rosecrans was removed. In fact, they were written by Charles Dana, not Garfield. On October 16, the day that Lincoln's cabinet met to discuss Rosecrans's fate, Dana sent a dispatch suggesting that Rosecrans was on the verge of abandoning Chattanooga and that even the general's staff was in favor of his dismissal: "I never saw anything which seemed so lamentable and hopeless. Nothing can prevent the retreat of the army from this place within a fortnight." Thus, it was damaging dispatches from Dana—not Garfield—that had contributed to Rosecrans's removal after Chickamauga. The belief that it was Garfield who doomed Rosecrans emerged from Chase's incorrect telling of the story to James Gilmore and the dubious accusations of Charles Dana, who was himself to blame in the matter of Rosecrans's dismissal.[246]

While Garfield had not secretly written to Washington to have Rosecrans removed from command, he did not wholeheartedly defend Rosecrans after Chickamauga. On his way home from the Army of the Cumberland, Garfield met Edwin Stanton in Louisville on October 21. There, with other officers, Stanton interviewed Garfield, asking him detailed questions about the Army of the Cumberland and Rosecrans's conduct at Chickamauga. No record exists stating exactly what Garfield did say to Stanton regarding Rosecrans, but what is known is that Stanton already had a strong disdain for the commander of the Army of the Cumberland. Just before speaking with Garfield, Stanton had heard Dana's opinion of Rosecrans's actions at Chickamauga, further augmenting his dislike for the general.[247]

According to Stanton, as well as General Anson Stager, who was also present at the meeting, Garfield denounced Rosecrans, giving a poor opinion of his commanding officer. As Stager later noted, Garfield said that Rosecrans had lost the confidence of the army "and should be removed." Stanton believed that he had the evidence he was seeking. He sent a message to Lincoln indicating that his interviews "more than confirm the worst that

177

has reached us as to the conduct of the commanding General and the great credit that is due Thomas."[248]

The time frame of Garfield's meeting with Stanton is important. While his testimony did not help Rosecrans, it came after Grant had issued orders for his removal. In his discussion with Stanton, as an army officer and a congressman-elect, it was Garfield's responsibility to speak earnestly about Rosecrans the army officer, not the man with whom Garfield had developed a close working friendship. As Jacob Cox later noted in his *Military Reminiscences of the Civil War,* Garfield was no longer Rosecrans's chief of staff, but he was still duty bound to provide Stanton his opinion on what had occurred at Chickamauga. He clearly did not believe that Rosecrans had performed well on September 20, 1863. Garfield would tell Rosecrans that he had defended him when speaking with Stanton, yet both the secretary of war and General Anson Stager thought otherwise.[249]

After Garfield met with Stanton, he continued on to Washington, where he met with the president. Despite his statements to the contrary, Garfield was still uncertain whether he wanted to take his seat in Congress or remain in the army. Lincoln assured him that leaving for Congress was the correct path to take because he desperately needed congressmen "who knew the wants of the armies from practical knowledge." It is not clear what Garfield may have said to Lincoln regarding Rosecrans at this time, but in December 1863, he wrote to Rosecrans to tell him that he had urged the president to place the general in the field once again, suggesting that Rosecrans could soon find himself assigned to the Department of the Missouri, which is where he ended up in 1864. Again in this instance, even if Garfield had told the president to remove Rosecrans (of which there is no reliable evidence), his meeting with Lincoln occurred after Rosecrans had been dismissed.

Nevertheless, many have doubted Garfield's account of his meeting with the president. According to Montgomery Blair, a Rosecrans supporter and political opponent of James Garfield, the young congressman-elect from Ohio had used this meeting to tell Lincoln of Rosecrans's allegedly poor performance at Chickamauga. Blair supposedly learned this in conversation with Lincoln himself. Seeing Garfield publicly defend Rosecrans at a dinner party hosted by his father, Francis Preston Blair, Montgomery Blair noted that he was "very much astonished at his duplicity."[250]

Blair's account, written in 1880 when Garfield was running for the presidency, is clouded both by the passage of time and the national spotlight of a presidential race. As evidence, Blair indicated to Rosecrans that

Garfield's meeting with Lincoln in which he had denounced the general occurred before Rosecrans was removed from command, which was not true. Thus, considering the timing of the account, Blair's version of events must be treated skeptically.[251]

It is clear that, while he served as the chief of staff for the Army of the Cumberland, James Garfield developed strong disagreements with William Rosecrans. Garfield was not shy in sharing these professional opinions through his letters with Salmon Chase and his meeting with Edwin Stanton. Certainly, his letters to Chase throughout 1863 discussed what Garfield perceived as Rosecrans's shortcomings as a commander, and they did not help the relationship between Rosecrans and Washington. Additionally, his conversation with Stanton did not provide a positive account of Rosecrans's actions at Chickamauga. However, considering the timing of his communications with Chase and Stanton, it does not appear as though he played a direct role in Rosecrans's dismissal after Chickamauga. His letters to Chase occurred before the battle, and his conversation with Stanton occurred several days after Rosecrans was removed. While Chase and Dana would later claim that Garfield had written critical letters after Chickamauga, no such letters appear to exist.[252]

From the time he first met the general, Garfield was personally loyal to Rosecrans, but his political beliefs, persuasions and passions in seeing the war against the Confederacy prosecuted vigorously fostered great frustration during Rosecrans's many prolonged periods of inaction. This frustration was widely held by many senior leaders of the Union army, especially those in the Lincoln administration in Washington. While Garfield's communications with Chase and Stanton may suggest that he was disloyal to Rosecrans, one important fact suggests otherwise. Garfield made no public utterances or published statements defaming or criticizing Rosecrans. Garfield's criticisms of the general came in private correspondence and conversations. He never publicly provided any recriminations of his commanding officer at Chickamauga. Even his meeting with Stanton was private, and Garfield did not write or speak publicly of it. Indeed, much of what we know regarding Garfield's private thoughts on Rosecrans at Chickamauga comes from Jacob Cox. After speaking with Stanton in Louisville, Garfield met with Cox in Cincinnati, speaking of the recent battle and his experiences there. Cox would later publish what Garfield had told him, though not until 1900, forty years after the war and twenty years after Garfield died. Certainly, this was not Garfield using a publication for his own personal benefit. Because of his deep personal admiration for Rosecrans, Garfield perhaps refrained from publicly speaking of the general's failures at Chickamauga so as not to further damage the reputation of his former commander. If his goal was to disparage Rosecrans for his own political benefit, this would be a strange course to take, no doubt.[253]

In February 1864, when Congress was considering a resolution thanking George Thomas for his efforts at Chickamauga, Garfield did rise to speak publicly on what he had seen at Chickamauga. Garfield spoke in opposition to the resolution, not because of any personal disregard for Thomas, but because it did not also praise Rosecrans. "On what grounds are you now ready to ignore the man who has won so many of your proudest victories?" Garfield asked the House. He rejected the idea that Chickamauga was a disaster, noting, "If that battle was a defeat we may welcome a hundred such defeats." He spoke of Chickamauga as part of a larger campaign for Chattanooga, taking care to state that the Confederates had held the advantage in numbers during the battle the previous September. At the end of the campaign, the Federals still held Chattanooga and the Confederates were south of the Tennessee River, which, as Garfield said, was Rosecrans's primary objective in the first place. "If there has been a more substantial success against overwhelming odds since the war began, I have not heard of it," Garfield proclaimed.

While clearly confusing the facts—he stated that the Confederates outnumbered the Federals seventy-five thousand to forty thousand—Garfield did not once defame Rosecrans's character or actions in his remarks. With the attention of Congress, just months after he had made his famous ride to Thomas, Garfield had the perfect opportunity to describe in great detail Rosecrans's confusing order to Thomas Wood that doomed the Union center and how he, not the commanding general, had made his way to Thomas to help save the day. As a member of the Committee on Military Affairs, it would have been within Garfield's purview to tell the tale of how badly Rosecrans had failed at Chickamauga, further elevating his own name by denigrating that of his former commander. Yet that is not the message Garfield delivered. In some of his only public remarks on Chickamauga, Garfield was true to his former commander:

> *After the disaster to the right wing in the last bloody afternoon of September 20th, twenty-five thousand men of the Army of the Cumberland stood and met seventy-five thousand men hurled against them. And they stood in their bloody tracks, immovable and victorious when night threw its mantle around them. They had repelled the last assault of the rebel army. Who commanded the Army of the Cumberland? Who organized, disciplined,*

and led it? Who planned its campaigns? The general whose name is omitted in this resolution, Major General W.S. Rosecrans.

Absent was any sarcasm or hints of bitterness. He said nothing of Rosecrans being unnerved, something that he did mention in private conversation to Jacob Cox and Henry Alden. Even if he believed Rosecrans had been too rattled to continue his command at Chickamauga, he said nothing of it publicly. Instead, he offered only praise for both George Thomas and William Rosecrans, men whom he knew exceedingly well from his time in the army: "If there is any man upon earth whom I honor it is the man who is named in this resolution, General George H. Thomas…I know, and all know, that he deserves well of his country, and his name ought to be recorded in letters of gold; but I know equally well that General Rosecrans deserves well of his country."[254]

Garfield's alleged role in the dismissal of William Rosecrans has certainly garnered its fair share of controversy. While many have suspected that he was duplicitous when it came to Rosecrans's removal, that was not the case. Garfield was a man who, because of his strong personal beliefs on how the war should be fought, came to have disagreements with his commanding officer. He privately shared these with Chase in the summer of 1863 and with Stanton in late October of that year once Rosecrans had been dismissed. Garfield never publicly defamed Rosecrans for his political benefit, which he certainly had the chance to do. Instead, when he did comment publicly, he praised Rosecrans for his service to the country. Garfield's relationship with Rosecrans was not perfect. He personally admired Rosecrans while still experiencing professional frustrations concerning his conduct. Garfield's actions are not those of someone scheming to tear down Rosecrans for his own personal gain but, rather, one who had conflicting emotions regarding Rosecrans and the role he was playing in the Civil War.

Garfield's 1868 Memorial Day Oration

In addition to being an educator, politician and army general, James Garfield was also a tremendous orator. Of all the speeches that he delivered during his life and career, perhaps none was as moving as a tribute he gave in 1868 to those who died during the Civil War. Before it was known as Memorial Day, the last Monday in May was known as Decoration Day. In the immediate aftermath of the Civil War, a practice began where citizens would decorate the graves of those who had died with flowers as a token of thanks for the sacrifices made for the continued existence of the nation. On May 30, 1868, Garfield delivered the following remarks at the graves of Union soldiers in Arlington, Virginia, on the former estate of Robert E. Lee, what is now Arlington National Cemetery. No piece of oratory is more emblematic of Garfield's classical education, his beautiful poetry and his belief and dedication to the cause of the Union as this speech.

Oration of Honorable James A. Garfield
Delivered at Arlington, VA, May 30, 1868
On the Occasion of
Strewing flowers on the graves of Union soldiers

Mr. President,

I am oppressed with a sense of the impropriety of uttering words on this occasion. If silence is ever golden, it must be here, beside the graves of fifteen thousand men, whose lives were more significant than speech, and whose death was a poem the music of which can never be sung. With words, we make promises, plight faith, praise virtue. Promises may not be kept; plighted faith may be broken; and vaunted virtue be only the cunning mask of vice. We do not know one promise these men made, one pledge they gave, one word they spoke; but we do know they summed up and perfected by one supreme act, the highest virtues of men and citizens. For love of country they accepted death; and thus resolved all doubts, and made immortal their patriotism and virtue.

For the noblest man that lives there still remains a conflict. He must still withstand the assaults of time and fortune; must still be assailed with temptations before which lofty natures have fallen. But with these, the conflict ended, the victory was won, when death stamped on them the great seal of heroic character, and closed a record which years can never blot.

I know of nothing more appropriate on this occasion than to inquire what brought these men here. What high motive led them to condense life into an hour, and to crown that hour by joyfully welcoming death? Let us consider.

Eight years ago, this was the most unwarlike nation of the earth. For nearly fifty years, no spot, in any of these states, had been the scene of battle. Thirty millions of people had an army of less than ten thousand men. The faith of our people in the stability and permanence of their institutions, was like their faith in the eternal course of nature. Peace, liberty and personal security, were blessings as common and universal as sunshine and showers and fruitful seasons; and all sprang from a single source—the principle declared in the Pilgrim covenant of 1620—that all owed due submission and obedience to the lawfully expressed will of the majority. This is not one of the doctrines of our political system—it is the system itself. It is our political firmament, in which all other truths are set, as stars in heaven. It is the encasing air; the breath of the nation's life. Against this principle the whole weight of the rebellion was thrown. Its overthrow would have brought such ruin as might follow in the physical universe, if the power of gravitation were destroyed and—

> *Nature's concord broke*
> *Among the constellations war were sprung.*
> *And planets, rushing from aspect malign*
> *Of fiercest opposition, in mid sky*
> *Should combat, and their jarring spheres confound.*

The nation was summoned to arms, by every high motive which can inspire men. Two centuries of freedom had made its people unfit for despotism. They must save their Government, or miserably perish.

As a flash of lightning in a midnight tempest reveals the abysmal horrors of the sea, so did the flash of the first gun disclose the awful abyss into which rebellion was ready to plunge us. In a moment, the fire was lighted in twenty million hearts. In a moment, we were the most warlike nation on the earth. In a moment, we were not merely a people with an army—we were a people in arms. The nation was in column—not all at the front, but all in the array.

I love to believe that no heroic sacrifice is ever lost; that the characters of men are moulded and inspired by what their fathers have done; that, treasured up in American souls, are all the unconscious influences of the great deeds of the Anglo-Saxon race, from Agincourt to Bunker Hill. It was such an influence that led a young Greek, two thousand years ago, when musing on the battle of Marathon, to exclaim, "The trophies of Miltiades will not let me sleep." Could these men be silent in 1861—these, whose ancestors had felt the inspiration of battle, on ever field where civilization had fought in the last thousand years? Read their answer in this green turf. Each for himself gathered up the cherished purposes of life—its aims and ambitions, its dearest affections—and flung all, with life itself, into the scale of battle.

We began the war for the Union alone; but we had not gone far into its darkness before a new element was added to the conflict, which filled the army and the nation with cheerful but intense religious enthusiasm. In lessons that could not be misunderstood, the Nation was taught that God had linked to our own, the destiny of an enslaved race—that their liberty and our Union were indeed "one and inseparable." It was this that made the soul of John Brown the marching companion of our soldiers, and made them sing as they went down to battle—

> *In the beauty of the lilies Christ was born, across the sea,*
> *With a glory in his bosom which transfigures you and me;*
> *As he died to make men holy, let us die to make men free;*
> *While God is marching on.*

With such inspirations, failure was impossible. The struggle consecrated, in some degree, every man who bore a worthy part. I can never forget an incident, illustrative of this thought, which it was my fortune to witness, near sunset of the second day at Chickamauga, when the beleaguered but unbroken left wing of our army had again and again repelled the assaults of more than double their numbers, and when each soldier felt that to his individual hands were committed the life of the army and the honor of his country. It was just after a division had fired its last cartridge, and had repelled a charge at the point of the bayonet, that the great-hearted commander took the hand of an humble soldier and thanked him for his steadfast courage. The soldier stood silent for a moment, and then said, with deep emotion, "George H. Thomas has taken this hand in his. I'll knock down any mean man that offers to take it hereafter." This rough sentence was full of meaning. He felt that something had happened to his hand which consecrated it. Could a hand bear our banner in battle and not be forever consecrated to honor and virtue? But doubly consecrated were these who received into their own hearts the fatal shafts, aimed at the life of their country. Fortunate men! Your country lives because you died! Your fame is placed where the breath of calumny can never reach it; where the mistakes of a weary life can never dim its brightness! Coming generations will rise up to call you blessed!

And now, consider this silent assembly of the dead. What does it represent? Nay, rather, what does it not represent? It is an epitome of the War. Here are sheaves reaped, in the harvest of death, from every battlefield of Virginia. If each grave had a voice to tell us what its silent tenant last saw and heard on earth, we might stand, with uncovered heads, and hear the whole story of the war. We should hear that one perished when the first great drops of the crimson shower began to fall, when the darkness of that first disaster at Manassas fell like an eclipse on the nation; that another died of disease while wearily waiting for winter to end; that this one fell on the field, in sight of the spires of Richmond, little dreaming that the flag must be carried through three more years of blood before it should be planted in that citadel of treason; and that one fell when the tide of war had swept us back, till the roar of rebel guns shook the dome of yonder Capitol, and re-echoed in the chambers of the Executive Mansion. We should hear mingled voices from the Rappahannock, the Rapidan, the Chickahominy, and the James; solemn voices from the Wilderness, and triumphant shouts from the Shenandoah, from Petersburg, and the Five Forks, mingled with the wild acclaim of victory and the sweet chorus of returning peace. The voices of these dead will forever fill the land like holy benedictions.

What other spot so fitting for their last resting-place as this, under the shadow of the Capitol saved by their valor? Here, where the grim edge of battle joined; here, where all the hope and fear and agony of their country centered; here let them rest, asleep on the nation's heart, entombed in the nation's love!

Appendix B

The view from this spot bears some resemblance to that which greets the eye at Rome. In sight of the Capitoline Hill, up and across the Tiber, and overlooking the city, is a hill, not rugged or lofty, but known as the Vatican Mount. At the beginning of the Christian Era, an Imperial circus stood on its summit. There, gladiator slaves died for the sport of Rome; and wild beasts fought with wilder men. In that arena, a Gallilean fisherman gave up his life a sacrifice for his faith. No human life was ever so nobly avenged. On that spot was reared the proudest Christian temple ever built by human hands. For its adornment, the rich offerings of every clime and kingdom have been contributed. And now, after eighteen centuries, the hearts of two hundred million people turn towards it with reverence when they worship God. As the traveler descends the Appenines, he sees the dome of St. Peter rising above the desolate Campaigns and the dead city, long before the seven hills and ruined palaces appear to his view. The fame of the dead fisherman has outlived the glory of the Eternal City. A noble life, crowned with heroic death rises above and outlives the pride and pomp and glory of the mightiest empire of the earth.

Seen from the western slope of our Capitol, in direction, distance, and appearance, this spot is not unlike the Vatican Mount; though the river that flows at our feet is larger than a hundred Tibers. Seven years ago, this was the home of one who lifted his sword against the life of his country, and who became the great Imperator of the rebellion. The soil beneath our feet was watered by the tears of slaves, in whose hearts the sight of yonder proud Capitol awakened no pride and inspired no hope. The face of the goddess that crowns it was turned towards the sea and not towards them. But, thanks be to God, this arena of rebellion and slavery is a scene of violence and crime no longer! This will be forever the sacred mountain of our Capital. Here is our temple; its pavement is the sepulcher of heroic hearts; its dome, the bending heaven; its altar candles, the watching stars.

Hither our children's children shall come to pay their tribute of grateful homage. For this are we met today. By the happy suggestion of a great society, assemblies like this are gathering at this hour, in every state in the Union. Thousands of soldiers are today turning aside in the march of life to visit the silent encampments of dead comrades who once fought by their side.

From many thousand homes, whose light was put out when a soldier fell, there go forth today, to join these solemn processions, loving kindred and friends, from whose hearts the shadow of grief will never be lifted till the light of the Eternal world dawns upon them.

APPENDIX B

And here are children, little children, to whom the war left no father but the Father above. By the most sacred rights, theirs is the chief place today. They come with garlands to crown their victor fathers. I will delay the coronation no longer.[255]

Notes

For more on sources related to the life and Civil War career of James Garfield, visit www.fieryordeal.blogspot.com.

Chapter 1

1. Theodore Clarke Smith, *The Life and Letters of James Abram Garfield* (Archon Books, 1968; repr., New Haven, CT: Yale University Press, 1925), 1:4 (all references hereafter are to volume one unless otherwise noted).
2. Ibid., 3–5; Allan Peskin, *Garfield* (1978; repr., Kent, OH: Kent State University Press, 1999), 5.
3. Peskin, *Garfield*, 8.
4. Ibid., 9
5. Ibid., 11.
6. Ibid., 14–16; Smith, *Life and Letters*, 27–31.
7. Peskin, *Garfield*, 17.
8. Smith, *Life and Letters*, 35; Peskin, *Garfield*, 17.
9. Peskin, *Garfield*, 22.
10. Smith, *Life and Letters*, 51.
11. Peskin, *Garfield*, 33–43.
12. Smith, *Life and Letters*, 95–96; Peskin, *Garfield*, 19.
13. Peskin, *Garfield*, 46.
14. Ibid., 54–55.
15. Ibid., 53–58.
16. Ibid., 59–61.
17. Ibid., 65.

18. Ibid.
19. Smith, *Life and Letters*, 142.
20. Adam Goodheart, *1861: The Civil War Awakening* (New York: Alfred A. Knopf, 2011), 118.

Chapter 2

21. Ibid., 98–99.
22. Eugene Schmeil, *Citizen General: Jacob Dolson Cox and the Civil War Era* (Athens: Ohio University Press, 2014), 6–9.
23. Ibid., 10.
24. Ibid., 12–16
25. Ibid., 16.
26. Maryl L. Hinsdale, ed., *Garfield-Hinsdale Letters: Correspondence Between James Abram Garfield and Burke Aaron Hinsdale* (Ann Arbor: University of Michigan Press, 1949), 48–49.
27. Peskin, *Garfield*, 70–71.
28. W.T. Bascom to Garfield, May 11, 1860, James A. Garfield Papers, Library of Congress (hereafter referred to as JAG Papers, LOC), Reel 10.
29. JAG Papers, LOC, Reel 126.
30. W.T. Bascom to JAG, June 15, 1860, JAG Papers, LOC, Reel 10.
31. JAG Papers, LOC, Reel 126.
32. Peskin, *Garfield*, 77.
33. Hinsdale, *Garfield-Hinsdale Letters*, 54–55.
34. W.B. Hazen to JAG, January 26, 1861, JAG Papers, LOC, Reel 11.
35. Peskin, *Garfield*, 80–81.
36. Goodheart, *1861*, 100–1.
37. Abraham Lincoln, *Collected Works of Abraham Lincoln*, edited by Roy P. Basler (New Brunswick, NJ: Rutgers University Press, 1953), 4: 205–6.
38. Goodheart, *1861*, 101–3; Smith, *Life and Letters*, 155.
39. Hinsdale, *Garfield-Hinsdale Letters*, 56–57.
40. Goodheart, *1861*, 133; James Bissland, *Blood, Tears, and Glory: How Ohioans Won the Civil War* (Wilmington, OH: Orange Frazer Press, 2007), 27.

Chapter 3

41. James A. Garfield, *The Wild Life of the Army: Civil War Letters of James A. Garfield*, edited by Frederick D. Williams (East Lansing: Michigan State University Press, 1964), 6.
42. Garfield, *Wild Life of the Army*, 6–7.
43. Bissland, *Blood, Tears, and Glory*, 72.

44. Smith, *Life and Letters*, 161; Daniel J. Ryan, *The Civil War Literature of Ohio: A Bibliography, with Explanatory and Historical Notes* (Cleveland, OH: Burrow Brothers, 1911), 141.

45. Garfield, *Wild Life of the Army*, 10–11.

46. Henry Spencer to JAG, May 3, 1861, JAG Papers, LOC.

47. *Weekly Portage Sentinel*, May 15, 1861.

48. G.B. Smith to JAG, May 4, 1861, JAG Papers, LOC; JAG to Lucretia, May 5, 1861, in Garfield, *Wild Life of the Army*, 14.

49. J.T. Smith to JAG, April 18, 1861, JAG Papers, LOC; John Clapp to JAG, April 17, 1861, in JAG Papers, LOC.

50. W.B. Hazen to JAG, May 1, 1861, May 14, 1861, JAG Papers, LOC.

51. Garfield, *Wild Life of the Army*, 16–17.

52. Bissland, *Blood, Tears, and Glory*, 132–33.

53. W.T. Bascom to JAG, June 21, 1861, JAG Papers, LOC, Reel 11.

54. Governor William Dennison to JAG, July 27, 1861, JAG Papers, LOC, Reel 11.

55. Garfield, *Wild Life of the Army*, 23.

56. Ibid., 23; W.T. Bascom to JAG, August 9, 1861, JAG Papers, LOC.

57. Peskin, *Garfield*, 93.

58. Ibid., 93–95.

59. Bissland, *Blood, Tears, and Glory*, 135; F.H. Mason, *The Forty-Second Ohio Infantry: A History of the Organization and Services of that Regiment in the War of the Rebellion* (Cleveland, OH: Cobb, Andrews, and Co. Publishers, 1876), 20.

60. James A. Garfield, "My Campaign in East Kentucky," *North American Review* (December 1886): 525.

61. J.D. Cox to JAG, November 8, 1861, JAG Papers, LOC, Reel 11.

62. Owen Johnston Hopkins, *Under the Flag of the Nation: Diaries and Letters of a Yankee Volunteer in the Civil War*, edited by Otto F. Bond (Columbus: Ohio State University Press, 1961), 12.

63. Smith, *Life and Letters*, 179; Mason, *Forty-Second Ohio Infantry*, 44; Hopkins, *Under the Flag of the Nation*, 13.

64. Mason, *Forty-Second Ohio Infantry*, 46.

Chapter 4

65. William Gienapp, "Abraham Lincoln and the Border States," *Journal of the Abraham Lincoln Association* 13, no. 1 (1992): 13.

66. Steven Woodworth, *Jefferson Davis and His Generals: The Failure of Confederate Command in the West* (Lawrence: University of Kansas Press, 1990), 53.

67. Gerald Prokopowicz, *All for the Regiment: The Army of the Ohio, 1861–1862* (Chapel Hill: University of North Carolina Press, 2001), 17.

68. Ezra J. Warner, *Generals in Blue: Lives of the Union Commanders* (1964, repr.; Baton Rouge: Louisiana State University Press, 1994), 51.

69. Earl Hess, *The War in the West: Victory and Defeat from the Appalachians to the Mississippi* (Chapel Hill: University of North Carolina Press, 2012), 29–30; Lincoln to Browning, September 22, 1861, in Lincoln, *Collected Works of Abraham Lincoln*, 4: 531.

70. For a full treatment of the Big Sandy Valley, see John David Preston, *The Civil War in the Big Sandy Valley of Kentucky*, 2nd ed. (Baltimore, MD: Gateway Press, 2008), 8–29.

71. Ezra J. Warner, *Generals in Gray: Lives of the Confederate Commanders* (1959; repr., Baton Rouge: Louisiana State University Press, 2006), 212–13.

72. Mason, *Forty-Second Ohio Infantry*, 12.

73. Ibid.; Garfield, "My Campaign in East Kentucky," 527; Peskin, *Garfield*, 101–2.

74. D.C. Buell to JAG, December 17, 1861, JAG Papers, LOC, Reel 11.

75. Garfield, "My Campaign in East Kentucky," 527–28; Mason, *Forty-Second Ohio Infantry*, 12; Preston, *Civil War in the Big Sandy Valley*, 57–58.

76. Garfield, *Wild Life of the Army*, 49–50.

77. Ibid., 52.

78. Hopkins, *Under the Flag of the Nation*, 14–15.

79. U.S. War Department, *Official Record of the War of the Rebellion*, ser. 1, vol. 7, pt. 1, 24–5 (hereafter referred to as *OR*; all citations are to series 1).

80. Preston, *Civil War in the Big Sandy Valley*, 62–63; Hopkins, *Under the Flag of the Nation*, 15–16; James M. Perry, *Touched with Fire: Five Presidents and the Civil War Battles that Made Them* (New York: Public Affairs, 2003), 67.

81. *OR*, 7, pt. 1, 26–27.

82. Peskin, *Garfield*, 111–12.

83. Ibid.; Perry, *Touched with Fire*, 76–77; *OR*, 7, pt. 1, 28.

84. Perry, *Touched with Fire*, 71.

85. *OR*, pt. 7, 1, 45; 52.

86. Perry, *Touched with Fire*, 76.

87. Preston, *Civil War in the Big Sandy Valley*, 70–72; *OR*, 7, pt. 1, 28.

88. Perry, *Touched with Fire*, 82; Joseph Bowker, *Memories of Company F, 42nd O.V.I.* (Columbus, OH: Glenn and Heide, 1864), 13.

89. Preston, *Civil War in the Big Sandy Valley*, 73.

90. Garfield, *Wild Life of the Army*, 57.

91. Hopkins, *Under the Flag of the Nation*, 18; Bowker, *Memories of Company F*, 13–14.

92. Perry, *Touched with Fire*, 85; Garfield, *Wild Life of the Army*, 59.

93. Garfield, *Wild Life of the Army*, 57.

94. Ibid., 59; Perry, *Touched with Fire*, 86; *OR*, 7, pt. 1, 31.

95. Garfield, *Wild Life of the Army*, 60–61; *OR*, 7, pt. 1, 30–32; Preston, *Civil War in the Big Sandy*, 77.

96. Bowker, *Memories of Company F*, 15; *OR*, 7, pt. 1, 31.

97. *OR*, 7, pt. 1, 31.

98. Ibid., 31–32; Preston, *Civil War in the Big Sandy Valley*, 79.

99. *OR*, 7, pt. 1, 47–48.

100. Ibid., 30–32.

101. Ibid., 49.

102. General Order Number 4, January 16, 1862, JAG Papers, LOC, Reel 129.

103. Preston, *Civil War in the Big Sandy Valley*, 81.

104. *OR*, 7, pt. 1, 55–58.

105. W.B. Hazen to JAG, January 15, 1862; D.C. Buell to JAG, January 20, 1862; David Tod to JAG, January 24, 1862, JAG Papers, LOC, Reel 12; Perry, *Touched with Fire*, 88.

106. JAG Papers, LOC, Reel 12. Albin Schoeff fought under Thomas at Mill Springs; General William Nelson had entered into the Sandy Valley in November 1861, weeks before Garfield; and Commodore A.H. Foote had commanded naval forces in Grant's expedition to seize Forts Henry and Donelson.

107. Mason, *Forty-Second Ohio Infantry*, 76.

CHAPTER 5

108. Bowker, *Memories of Company F*, 17; Hopkins, *Under the Flag of the Nation*, 19; Preston, *Civil War in the Big Sandy Valley*, 98–100.

109. Preston, *Civil War in the Big Sandy Valley*, 99; Hopkins, *Under the Flag of the Nation*, 19–20; Bowker, *Memories of Company F*, 17; Smith, *Life and Letters*, 198–99.

110. Garfield, *Wild Life of the Army*, 67–68.

111. Ibid., 74–75.

112. Ibid., 65–66.

113. Smith, *Life and Letters*, 197.

114. February 3, 1862, Ohio State Senate Resolution, JAG Papers, LOC, Reel 12.

115. Smith, *Life and Letters*, 201; Salmon P. Chase, *Inside Lincoln's Cabinet: The Civil War Diaries of Salmon P. Chase*, edited by David Donald (New York: Longmans, Green and Co., 1954), 160.

116. Preston, *Civil War in the Big Sandy Valley*, 105–9.

117. James D. Norris and James K. Martin, eds., "Three Civil War Letters of James A. Garfield," *Ohio History Journal* 9, no. 4 (Autumn 1965): 250.

118. Thomas Tompkins Papers, HCWRT Collection, U.S. Army Heritage Education Center, Carlisle, PA (hereafter USAHEC).

119. Timothy Smith, *Shiloh: Conquer or Perish* (Lawrence: University Press of Kansas, 2014), 75–76.

120. Ibid., 145–47.

121. Thomas Tompkins Papers, USAHEC.

122. Ibid.; Norris and Martin, "Three Civil War Letters of James A. Garfield," 250.

123. *OR*, 10, pt. 1, 380; Norris and Martin, "Three Civil War Letters of James A. Garfield," 250.

124. Smith, *Conquer or Perish*, 247.

125. Garfield, *Wild Life of the Army*, 81–83.

126. Ibid., 105.

127. Norris and Martin, "Three Civil War Letters of James A. Garfield," 251.

128. Peskin, *Garfield*, 139; Garfield, *Wild Life of the Army*, 90.

129. Garfield, *Wild Life of the Army*, 111.

130. Ibid., 112, 119.

131. Peskin, *Garfield*, 144–45.

132. JAG to Swaim, July 20, 1862, in David Swaim Letters, MS. 3263, Western Reserve Historical Society (hereafter WRHS).

CHAPTER 6

133. JAG Papers, LOC, Reel 12.

134. Peskin, *Garfield*, 146; Garfield, *Wild Life of the Army*, 144.

135. Smith, *Life and Letters*, 233; Garfield, *Wild Life of the Army*, 133–35.

136. Smith, *Life and Letters*, 222.

137. JAG Papers, LOC, Reel 12.

138. Peskin, *Garfield*, 147; Smith, *Life and Letters*, 235.

139. Hinsdale, *Garfield-Hinsdale Letters*, 60–62.

140. Garfield, *Wild Life of the Army*, 65.

141. Ibid., 140.

142. Union general Phil Kearney was killed on September 1, 1862, at the Battle of Chantilly.

143. Margaret Leech and Harry J. Brown, *The Garfield Orbit* (New York: Harper and Row, 1978), 123; Garfield, *Wild Life of the Army*, 153–55.

144. John J. Hennessy, "Fitz John Porter and the Union War, 1862," in *Corps Commanders in Blue: Union Major Generals in the Civil War*, edited by Ethan Rafuse (Baton Rouge: Louisiana State University Press, 2015), 14–48, 37.

145. Peter Cozzens, *General John Pope: A Life for the Nation* (Urbana: University of Illinois Press, 2000), 147–49. For a detailed account of the Battle of Second

Manassas, see John J. Hennessy, *Return to Bull Run: The Campaign and Battle of Second Manassas* (Norman: University of Oklahoma Press, 1999).

146. Hennessy, *Return to Bull Run*, 463–67; Cozzens, *General John Pope*, 198.

147. Peskin, *Garfield*, 633.

148. Garfield, *Wild Life of the Army*, 148, 306–16; Otto Eisenschiml, *The Celebrated Case of Fitz John Porter: An American Dreyfus Affair* (Indianapolis, IN: Bobbs-Merrill Company, 1950), 81.

149. Cozzens, *General John Pope*, 217–18.

150. Garfield, *Wild Life of the Army*, 195, 199.

151. Ibid., 212–13; Cozzens, *General John Pope*, 224.

152. Hennessy, "Fitz John Porter and the Union War," 44–48.

153. Peskin, *Garfield*, 164; Eisenschiml, *Celebrated Case of Fitz John Porter*, 262, 310.

Chapter 7

154. Not many biographies have been written on Rosecrans, but by far the best is William Lamers, *The Edge of Glory: A Biography of General William S. Rosecrans, U.S.A.* (1961; repr., Baton Rouge: Louisiana State University Press, 1999).

155. Garfield, *Wild Life of the Army*, 225–28.

156. Ibid.

157. Larry Daniel, *Days of Glory: The Army of the Cumberland, 1861–1865* (Baton Rouge: Louisiana State University Press, 2004), 228; JAG to Chase, January 1863, in James A. Garfield Family Papers, MS. 4575, WRHS; Garfield, *Wild Life of the Army*, 233–34.

158. JAG to Chase, February 15, 1863, in Garfield Family Papers, MS. 4575, WRHS.

159. JAG Papers, LOC, Reel 12.

160. Garfield, *Wild Life of the Army*, 118.

161. Hess, *War in the West*, 178; Daniel, *Days of Glory*, 278.

162. Garfield to Chase, Garfield Family Papers, MS. 4575, WRHS.

163. Daniel, *Days of Glory*, 242.

164. Steven Woodworth, *Six Armies in Tennessee: The Chickamauga and Chattanooga Campaigns* (Lincoln: University of Nebraska Press, 1998), 17.

165. *OR*, 23, pt. 2, 395, 420; James R. Gilmore, *Personal Recollections of Abraham Lincoln and the Civil War* (1898; repr., Mechanicsburg, PA: Stackpole Books, 2007), 125.

166. Daniel, *Days of Glory*, 260; Lamers, *Edge of Glory*, 270.

167. Garfield, *Wild Life of the Army*, 275.

168. *OR*, 23, pt. 2, 420–24.

169. Daniel, *Days of Glory*, 264; Whitelaw Reid, *Ohio in the War: Her Statesmen, Her Generals and Soldiers* (New York: Moore, Wilstach, and Baldwin, 1868), 1: 752–53.

170. Daniel, *Days of Glory*, 264; Reid, *Ohio in the War*, 1: 757.

171. Daniel, *Days of Glory*, 265–74; Woodworth, *Six Armies in Tennessee*, 19–42.

172. Garfield, *Wild Life of the Army*, 285–86.

173. Lamers, *Edge of Glory*, 279; Daniel, *Days of Glory*, 273.

174. Christopher L. Kolakowski, *The Stones River and Tullahoma Campaigns: This Army Does Not Retreat* (Charleston, SC: The History Press, 2011), 134–35.

175. Lamers, *Edge of Glory*, 289–90.

176. *OR*, 23, pt. 2, 518.

Chapter 8

177. Woodworth, *Six Armies in Tennessee*, 52.

178. *OR*, 23, pt. 2, 552–55.

179. Garfield to Chase, July 27, 1863, in Garfield Family Papers, MS. 4575, WRHS.

180. Garfield, *Wild Life of the Army*, 291.

181. Daniel, *Days of Glory*, 279.

182. Woodworth, *Six Armies in Tennessee*, 59–61.

183. Garfield, *Wild Life of the Army*, 292–93.

184. Ibid., 294.

185. Woodworth, *Six Armies in Tennessee*, 62–63.

186. Daniel, *Days of Glory*, 300.

187. William Lee White, *Bushwhacking on a Grand Scale: The Battle of Chickamauga, September 18–20, 1863* (El Dorado Hills, CA: Savas Beatie, 2013), 4; Woodworth, *Six Armies in Tennessee*, 49–52.

188. Woodworth, *Six Armies in Tennessee*, 67–74; Daniel, *Days of Glory*, 302–4.

189. Daniel, *Days of Glory*, 303; *OR*, 30, pt. 3, 564.

190. Daniel, *Days of Glory*, 310; Lamers, *Edge of Glory*, 320–21.

191. Garfield, *Wild Life of the Army*, 295–96.

192. David A. Powell, *The Chickamauga Campaign: A Mad Irregular Battle: From the Crossing of the Tennessee River through the Second Day, August 22–September 19, 1863* (El Dorado Hills, CA: Savas Beatie, 2014), 270; Woodworth, *Six Armies in Tennessee*, 84–85.

193. Peter Cozzens, *This Terrible Sound: The Battle of Chickamauga* (Urbana: University of Illinois Press, 1996), 417; Powell, *Chickamauga Campaign*, 270–75; Woodworth, *Six Armies in Tennessee*, 86.

194. Smith, *Life and Letters*, 324; Powell, *Chickamauga Campaign*, 358–59; Cozzens, *This Terrible Sound*, 139–40; JAG Papers, LOC, Reel 123/Vol. 5.

195. Woodworth, *Six Armies in Tennessee*, 87.

196. Ibid., 91–93; Daniel, *Days of Glory*, 318–20.

197. Lamers, *Edge of Glory*, 334–35; White, *Bushwhacking on a Grand Scale*, 67.

198. Woodworth, *Six Armies in Tennessee*, 103.

199. Lamers, *Edge of Glory*, 336; Daniel, *Days of Glory*, 324.

200. Cozzens, *This Terrible Sound*, 360–61.

201. Ibid., 51–52, 360–65; White, *Bushwhacking on a Grand Scale*, 100–1.

202. Cozzens, *This Terrible Sound*, 363; "Report of the Military Services of James A. Garfield," JAG Papers, LOC, Reel 122.

203. Charles Dana, *Recollections of the Civil War: With the Leaders at Washington and in the Field in the Sixties* (New York: D. Appleton and Company, 1913), 115; William Shanks, *Personal Recollections of Distinguished Generals* (New York: Harper and Brothers Publishers, 1866), 263.

204. Dana, *Recollections of the Civil War*, 115; Lamers, *Edge of Glory*, 351–52.

205. Cozzens, *This Terrible Sound*, 402–5.

206. Daniel, *Days of Glory*, 331; Cozzens, *This Terrible Sound*, 402–5; Smith, *Life and Letters*, 337–38; Peskin, *Garfield*, 208–9; Theodore Clarke Smith, "General Garfield at Chickamauga," *Massachusetts Historical Society Proceedings, October 1914–June 1915* (Boston: Massachusetts Historical Society, 1915), 48: 275–76; Henry Alden to JAG, March 7, 1867, JAG Papers, Reel 12.

207. Smith, *Life and Letters*, 337; Cozzens, *This Terrible Sound*, 468–69; *OR*, 30, pt. 1, 872.

208. *OR*, 30, pt. 1, 253; Frank Moore, *The Rebellion Record: A Diary of American Events, with Documents, Narratives, Illustrative Incidents, Poetry, Etc.* (New York: Van Nostrand, 1864), 7: 416; Peskin, *Garfield*, 210.

209. *OR*, 30, pt. 1, 856, 695.

210. Ibid., 141.

211. Woodworth, *Six Armies in Tennessee*, 129; Henry M. Cist, *The Army of the Cumberland* (New York: Charles Scribner's Sons, 1909), 226.

212. Cozzens, *This Terrible Sound*, 470–71; Woodworth, *Six Armies in Tennessee*, 127–29.

213. James Garfield, "Oration on the Life and Character of George H. Thomas," in *Society of the Army of the Cumberland: Fourth Reunion, Cleveland, 1870* (Cincinnati, OH: Robert Clarke, Co., 1870), 84.

214. *OR*, 30, pt. 1, 144–45.

215. Ibid., 146–48.

216. Woodworth, *Six Armies in Tennessee*, 130; Cozzens, *This Terrible Sound*, 479.

217. Cozzens, *This Terrible Sound*, 534–35.

218. Garfield, *Wild Life of the Army*, 298.

219. Peskin, *Garfield*, 211; Woodworth, *Six Armies in Tennessee*, 137–38.

220. Woodworth, *Six Armies in Tennessee*, 144; Peter Cozzens, *Shipwreck of Their Hopes: The Battles for Chattanooga* (Urbana: University of Illinois Press, 1996), 11; George Lewis, *The Campaigns of the 124ᵗʰ Ohio Volunteer Infantry, with Roster and Roll of Honor* (Akron, OH: Werner, 1894), 78.
221. JAG Papers, LOC, Reel 122.
222. *OR*, 30, pt. 4, 389–90.
223. Woodworth, *Six Armies in Tennessee*, 148–49; October 16, 1863 orders to Ulysses S. Grant, JAG Papers, LOC, Reel 122.
224. Peskin, *Garfield*, 218–19.
225. Garfield, *Wild Life of the Army*, 298.
226. Russell Conwell, *The Life, Speeches, and Public Services of James A. Garfield* (Boston: B.B. Russell, 1881), 172; JAG Papers, LOC, Reel 122.
227. JAG to David Swaim, December 15, 1863, in Garfield Family Papers, MS. 4575, WRHS.

CHAPTER 9

228. Peskin, *Garfield*, 224.
229. James A. Garfield, *The Works of James Abram Garfield*, edited by Burke A. Hinsdale (Cleveland, OH: Cobb, Andrews, and Co., 1882), 1: 1–18.
230. Ibid., 19–34.
231. Peskin, *Garfield*, 236–38.
232. JAG Papers, LOC, Reel 126.
233. Smith, *Life and Letters*, 383.
234. Conwell, *Life, Speeches, and Public Services*, 218–19.
235. Candice Millard, *Destiny of the Republic: A Tale of Madness, Medicine, and the Murder of a President* (New York: Doubleday, 2011), 29.
236. James Garfield, "The Teachings of a Soldier's Monument," in *James A. Garfield: His Speeches at Home, 1880*, edited by C.S. Carpenter (Oneonta, NY: C.S. Carpenter, 1880).
237. Garfield, *Works of James Abram Garfield*, 2: 789–90.
238. Millard, *Destiny of the Republic*, 140, 228.
239. Garfield National Memorial Committee, *The Man and the Mausoleum: Dedication of the Garfield Memorial Structure in Cleveland, Ohio, May 30, 1890* (Cleveland, OH: Cleveland Printing and Publishing Co., 1890), 21, 53.
240. Peskin, *Garfield*, 119.
241. Sergeant Oates, *Prison Life in Dixie* (Chicago: Central Book Concern, 1880), 199–205.
242. JAG Papers, LOC, Reel 126.

APPENDIX A

243. These arguments against Garfield are encapsulated perfectly in a recent work by Frank Varney on how Ulysses S. Grant and others have shaped our understanding of William Rosecrans. Frank Varney, *General Grant and the Rewriting of History: How the Destruction of William S. Rosecrans Influenced Our Understanding of the Civil War* (El Dorado Hills, CA: Savas Beatie, 2013).

244. Lamers, *Edge of Glory*, 408–9; Society of the Army of the Cumberland, *Burial of General Rosecrans, Arlington National Cemetery, May 17, 1902* (Cincinnati: Robert Clarke Company, 1903), 98.

245. Society of the Army of the Cumberland, *Burial of General Rosecrans*, 97.

246. Daniel, *Days of Glory*, 351.

247. Varney, *General Grant and the Rewriting of History*, 215–16; Lamers, *Edge of Glory*, 411.

248. Lamers, *Edge of Glory*, 411.

249. Peskin, *Garfield*, 217; Lamers, *Edge of Glory*, 411; Jacob Cox, *Military Reminiscences of the Civil War* (New York: Charles Scribner and Sons, 1900), 2: 10.

250. Lamers, *Edge of Glory*, 412–13.

251. Peskin, *Garfield*, 215.

252. Ibid., 217–18.

253. Cox, *Military Reminiscences*, 2: 10.

254. JAG Papers, LOC, Reel 126.

APPENDIX B

255. Ibid.

Index

About the Author

Courtesy of Caitlin Kostic.

Daniel J. Vermilya is a Civil War historian who currently works as a park ranger at Gettysburg National Military Park. He has previously worked at Antietam National Battlefield in Maryland, where he is also a licensed battlefield guide. He received his BA in history and politics from Hillsdale College in 2009 and his MA in history from John Carroll University in 2011. In 2012, he was awarded the first Joseph L. Harsh Memorial Scholar Award by the Save Historic Antietam Foundation. He is a native of Kirtland, Ohio, and has previously worked as a volunteer for the James A. Garfield National Historic Site. He currently lives in Frederick, Maryland, with his wife, Alison, and their pet rabbit, Clara. He is also the author of *The Battle of Kennesaw Mountain*, published in 2014 by The History Press.

Daniel maintains a blog on the American Civil War (www.fieryordeal. blogspot.com), as well as a blog site devoted to his book on the Battle of Kennesaw Mountain (www.kennesawmountain.wordpress.com).